the people's architect

carol ross barney

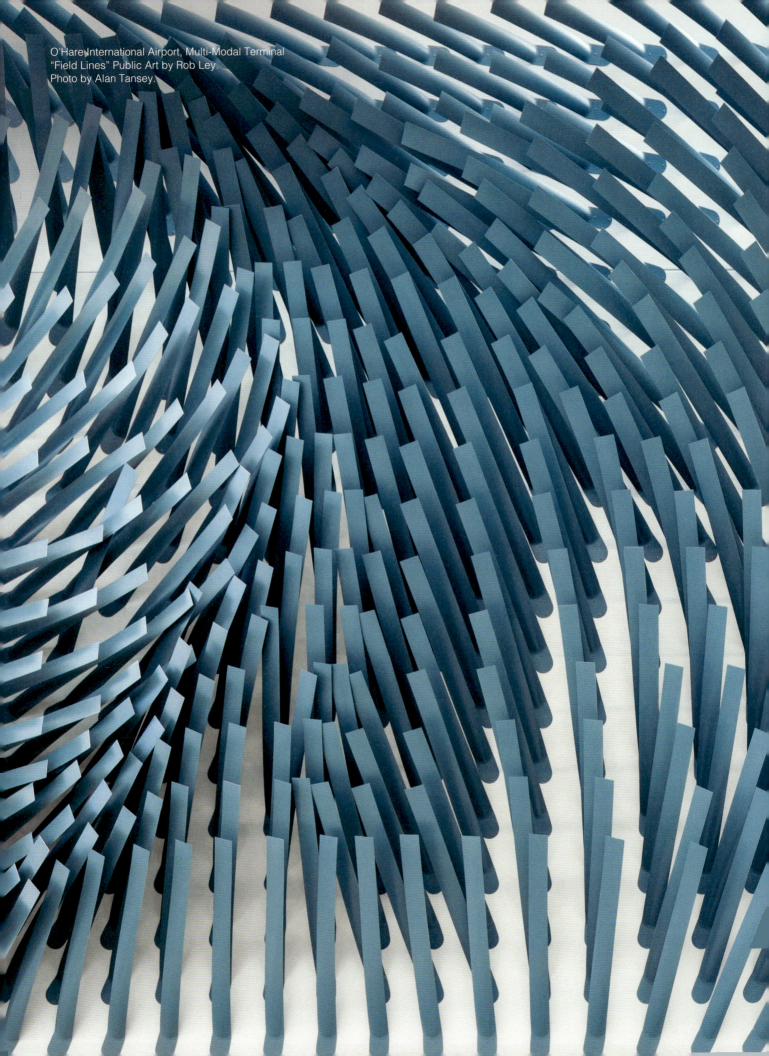

O'Hare International Airport, Multi-Modal Terminal "Field Lines" Public Art by Rob Ley. Photo by Alan Tansey.

the people's architect
carol ross barney

Introduction by Iker Gil
Edited by Oscar Riera Ojeda
Principal Photography by
Kate Joyce Studios,
Ross Barney Architects,
and Kendall McCaugherty,
Hall+Merrick+McCaugherty

OSCAR RIERA OJEDA
PUBLISHERS

"An unrivaled architect for the people, Barney exudes design excellence, social responsibility, and generosity. Throughout all of her work, she has endeavored to make the world a better place."

The American Institute of Architects, 2023 Gold Medal Citation

Photo by: John Boehm

Lincoln Park Zoo, Searle Visitor Center.
Photo by Kendall McCaugherty.

Contents

12	Introduction
16	The Future of Cities
23	Selected Work
24	Designing Democracy
74	Infrastructure of Hope
136	Repairing the World
184	Annex
186	Awards & Publications
190	Life Story
194	Studio Members
196	Contributors
197	Photography Credits
200	Book Credits

Introduction
by Iker Gil

Designing Our Cities with People in Mind

I am a firm believer that architects must contribute to our society in positive ways. Through their conceptual ideas and built work, and in collaboration with many others, they can advance the conversation about the evolving and complex futures of our cities. Carol Ross Barney and her studio, Ross Barney Architects, provide a clear path for those wanting to practice with dignity, care, equity, and collectivity in mind. Defined as the "people's architect" by the *Chicago Tribune Magazine* two decades ago,[1] Carol works in a wide range of scales and across typologies, always thoughtful, determined, and empathetic. One can identify a common thread across her diverse work and that is a focus on people at its core. Humanity is present in the projects she has designed, from riverwalks and transit stations to educational, civic, and commercial buildings.

Rivers are the backbone of cities around the world. They are the reason why people settled there in the first place, providing access to natural resources, fostering trade, and generating wealth to some sectors of the population. Rivers also exemplify an often-complicated relationship between city residents and this natural system, one in which economic benefits outweigh civic benefits. Chicago is one of those cities. Since the Potawatomi inhabited the area in the eighteenth century, the river has played a crucial role in the development of the Chicago that we see today. However, with the relocation of industries and docks to areas further from the center of the city over the decades, the role of this industrial waterway has evolved but often failed to live up to its potential as a civic space.

I grew up in a city that, despite differences in many other aspects, shared the same relationship with its river: instead of the backbone of the city, it had become a scar for most of the twentieth century. Bilbao's Nervión River (known as La Ría in its portion as an estuary) provided wealth at the expense of civic potential for its citizens. Industrial uses along the riverbanks, lack of physical connection between both banks, and serious environmental issues established this waterway as a physical and perceived barrier. Luckily, over the last twenty-five years, through large-scale projects in some areas and surgical interventions in others, Bilbao has been able to turn this scar into a civic space that has stitched together both banks of the river.

Over the last two decades, Chicago has also been able to rethink what kind of relationship it wants to have with its river, at least in the area around the Loop. With Lake Michigan as its celebrated front yard, what kind of role could the Chicago River play in the twenty-first-century city? Luckily, Chicago has an architect like Carol who, building upon ideas floated since the 1909 Plan of Chicago, was able to envision what was possible and had the drive, endurance, and commitment to make it happen over more than a decade. No small feat when working on a public project of this scale and prominence in a city like Chicago.

In a purposefully created 25-foot-wide space with under-bridge connections that required congressional approval, this tight civic space called the Chicago Riverwalk has created an uninterrupted connection between Lake Michigan and the confluence of the main, north, and south branches of the Chicago River. Along the one-and-a-quarter-mile-long space developed in three phases, one finds different "rooms" with carefully considered designs, unique programs, breathtaking views, reduced noise pollution, and proximity to the water. It is not just a space to connect point A to point B but a place of leisure, celebration, observation, and rediscovery.

Over the years, it has been remarkable to see how the physical transformation of this thin edge has changed our perception of and relationship with the river, from an infrastructural system to one of civic pride. Besides the programmed commercial spaces, you can see people jogging or on a slow stroll, walking their dogs, eating lunch alone on the steps or picnicking with friends on the lawn, taking photos, sunbathing, reading, fishing, and even racing RC boats. You don't have to pay a fee or consume in a designated establishment to access or enjoy this space. And it is not only remarkable what happens on the shore but also what happens in the river itself.

If two decades ago industrial barges were the most prominent users of the river, along with boat tours and water taxis, now all share space with rental electric boats, yachts of all sizes, kayak tours, and all kinds of recreational activities. Now that we have seen how this portion of the river edge could be reimagined, an example has been set to lead the way for other areas of the city by the Chicago River to receive the same care, focus, and resources.

The conceptual approach, design, and implementation of this project illustrates ways we can shape our cities for a better future. Carol has applied the idea that excellence in design is a human right since the start of her career. Regardless of clients, budgets, and typologies, good design is a right. And good design can be applied to high profile projects, such as the Chicago Riverwalk, as well as the most mundane of programs. That is exemplified by her early work redesigning Illinois Bell Telephone Co. remote switching facilities. While accessed occasionally by technicians but seen by many while driving, a typically unplanned functional structure dotting the landscape was here turned into a sculptural object. It was a declaration of intentions: build with dignity regardless of how mundane a project might appear.

There is nothing mundane about designing a public school, and Carol has designed several. Her Cesar Chavez Multicultural Academic Center, completed in the early 1990s in the Back of the Yards neighborhood of Chicago, demonstrated the importance of using architecture to celebrate community and, in this case, education. With a tight budget and a complicated site, Carol and her team created an efficient building with bold geometric forms and bright colors that stood out from its context and brought a sense of excitement. It not only broke out of its context for its color and geometry but also out of the standardized school design prevalent in Chicago, celebrating a unique identity, culture, and community.

Little Village Academy followed soon after with a different design but guided by the same principles. These uplifting buildings are bold statements of an unequivocal commitment to education and communities in working-class neighborhoods. They also demonstrate that by thinking in unique ways, the constraints we work with can produce a more elevated result than the norm.

If these schools work at a neighborhood and at a city scale, sometimes the design of a public building needs to be able to reassure us of something as important as our government and our values. These buildings might not be the ones that are defined in superlatives, but they are the ones that bring us confidence, comfort, and inspiration in moments of need. This is the case of the Oklahoma City Federal Building that Ross Barney Architects completed in 2005, a project that came about after the 1995 terrorist attack. Within that context of tragedy and mourning, the design approach begs the question: How do we move forward? How do we manage fear and design a secure space while aiming for openness and a will to welcome the city, its residents, and its workers?

These are not aspects that are easy to reconcile. Here, a building and a nearby park are stitched together by an elliptical space that defines a generous and protected courtyard, providing space for the community to gather. Other design aspects, such as the selection of materials, are carefully considered so that the building meets security requirements while avoiding the need to create a bunker-like structure. Carol has worked on many other public buildings that don't have the same symbolic role as the Oklahoma City Federal Building, but projects such as the Glendale Heights Post Office and the Champaign Public Library also incorporate all the pragmatic requirements while elevating the experience of those engaging with the buildings.

Sometimes it is not our public buildings that need to communicate that we need do things differently for a better world. McDonald's is the largest fast food restaurant chain in the world, with over 40,000 locations and more than $23 billion in revenue in 2021. At this scale, even the smallest change can have a large impact. In Chicago and Walt Disney World, Carol has been able to design two flagship McDonald's that challenge our assumptions of the ubiquitous experience of consuming a fast-food item. Both use similar strategies with different formal outcomes: a large canopy clad in solar panels that unifies the different elements of the project, materials with low-embodied energy, passive strategies to reduce energy needs, and a transparent façade that creates a sense of openness and connection to its context.

In the case of Chicago, this is particularly interesting as the site is in a block of the River North neighborhood surrounded by major roads. With investment in the public space outside the building and a focus on improving the pedestrian experience, this building also becomes a small respite in this fast-moving area of the city. It remains to be seen how much these strategies will be implemented in other McDonald's across the world, but these two flagship projects designed by Ross Barney Architects are not only showing what could theoretically be done; they are built and ready to be tested, evaluated, and discussed to advance the conversation about what and how we build. They demonstrate that we can be as sustainable as possible while still creating memorable experiences. We can build architecture.

These memorable experiences should also be expected in the infrastructure of our cities, whether it is subway systems, multimodal buildings, trail conversions, or even riverwalks like the one in Chicago. However, in many cases, architects are relegated to very minor roles or are not even part of the teams involved in these projects. This is a particular area where Carol's commitment has been influential in shaping the next generation of transportation projects in the city.

The work that Carol has done for the Chicago Transit Authority (CTA) not only has modernized and dignified their stations but has also provided recognizable structures that contribute to the development of neighborhoods. The new stations have become the brand for CTA. Whether it's the Morgan Street station in West Loop, the Cermak-McCormick Place station on the Near South Side, or the Belmont Gateway in Avondale, each in their own unique way has become a recognizable element in the neighborhood.

The Morgan Street station, completed in 2012 and the first new station in Chicago in twenty years, has a narrow footprint, but its towers, housing the stairs and elevators, give it a memorable presence in this rapidly changing neighborhood. The perforated façades allow daylight and a sense of transparency while at night, the towers become a beacon for the area. This care for a new element of daily infrastructure is a positive sign as we think about what city are we building. The trains might not come more often, but the experience of waiting for a train or encountering the station while walking on the sidewalk has been noticeably elevated. Public infrastructure matters. The people that take public infrastructure matter. How public infrastructure presents itself in the built environment matters. As Bogotá's former mayor Enrique Peñalosa has mentioned in multiple interviews, "an advanced city is one where the rich take public transportation."

Since starting her office in 1981, Carol and her studio have been able to contribute to making our cities, and Chicago in particular, more equitable, dignified, and human. When we look at the projects included in this book, we see what architecture can do, and how architects are capable of contributing to our society and to the conversation about the future of our cities. When thinking about the city of the future, some might be tempted to imagine it based on the latest fad or the latest technology or some landmark for few to have access to, but ultimately, the projects designed with dignity, care, equity, and collectivity in mind will be the ones that have a long-lasting impact in our cities.

The 2023 AIA Gold Medal was recognition of the steady excellence of the work done by Carol and her team over more than four decades. It has also brought their work and their approach to the forefront, inviting others to take on the baton. Cities will continue to evolve, be challenged, and be presented with new opportunities. It is not easy. It won't be easy. Carol's design excellence and relentless commitment to our cities is something we can all learn from. After all, there is a reason why Carol Ross Barney is The People's Architect.

Iker Gil
Founding Partner, MAS Studio
Founder, MAS Context
Executive Director, SOM Foundation

[1] Charles Leroux, "The People's Architect," Chicago Tribune Magazine, May 30, 2004.

CTA Cermak/McCormick Place Station.
Photo by Kate Joyce Studios.

The Future of Cities

"My dreams are for the future of cities... places where we live together. I want to help us understand the transformative effect space has on human interaction. Good design is a right, not a privilege."

Carol Ross Barney, FAIA, Honorary ASLA has been in the vanguard of civic space design since founding Ross Barney Architects in 1981. With a career that spans over 50 years, Carol has made significant contributions to the built environment, the profession, and architectural education. From her early days in the United States Peace Corps planning National Parks in Costa Rica to collaborations with Governments, Carol has relentlessly advocated that excellent design is a right, not a privilege.

Her body of work, being almost exclusively in the public realm, represents these aspirations and occupies a unique place within the panorama of contemporary architecture.

Carol's projects vary in type and scale, but always uphold a deep commitment to the quality of life. This commitment manifests into spaces that enrich the metropolitan experience; buildings that are environmental stewards, embodying and showcasing sustainability; and spaces that inspire young, curious minds to learn, invent, and break boundaries.

Carol's portfolio expresses an unpretentious appreciation of often forgotten buildings and infrastructure, the lifeblood of our cities, showing how they can be united through design.

To date she has realized a remarkable succession of compelling projects. Each takes on a honed process of giving voice to all members of a community. It is the ability to listen with intention to the history, context, and aspirations of a community first, and then respond. It is a story, told through design, about fairness, equity, and inspiration. No matter the scope or scale, each project explores an inventive and integrated approach to stewardship, whether that be to its neighbors or the environment; anything less is not an option.

By creating a place for people and ideas to come together, architecture becomes a medium for experiences to be shared and memories to be made.

left Photo of Carol Ross Barney working in a design charrette.
above The Bloomingdale Trail/606 brought people of all ages to engagement sessions, planning the future of their public space.
below Photo of Carol Ross Barney on the Chicago Riverwalk: Photo by Whitten Sabbatini

Carol has taught as an Adjunct Professor at the Illinois Institute of Technology in Chicago, Illinois, for over thirty years. Research topics have been interrelated with active architectural explorations; water transportation, equitable mixed used developments, material innovations such as heavy timber, and floating markets. Her popular advanced design studio at IIT has garnered interest from a wide cross section of undergraduate and graduate students in Architecture, Urbanism, and Landscape Architecture.

above Ross Barney Architects Studio, Photo by Tara White
below Photo of Cesar Chavez Multicultural Academic Center, courtesy of Ross Barney Architects

This commitment to education has embedded a generation of architects with Carol's philosophy of designing for people while driving the importance of adapting sustainable systems.

Selected Teaching Experience:
Adjunct Professor,
Illinois Institute of Technology, 1993-present
Pelli Distinguished Lecturer, University of Illinois, 2022
Bruce Goff Chair of Creative Architecture,
University of Oklahoma, 2002
Adjunct Assistant Professor of Architecture,
University of Illinois at Chicago, 1976-1978

At the forefront for equity in the architectural profession, Carol has long sought to move beyond her gender as a contributing factor or hindrance to success. But it's not enough just to blaze the trail, Carol continually teaches, mentors, and empowers young architects to contribute their ideas and designs to progress the profession.

Her focus on social justice and public good has attracted a dedicated group of architects to her studio that includes women (approximately half) and minorities (approximately half: 10% are African American, 8% Latinx, 25% Asian). This is more notable when considering that, according to a recent AIA member study, only 15% of licensed architects are female and 1-2% are of minority heritage.

Her studio includes native speakers of Spanish, Japanese, and Korean; immigrants and the native born; African-Americans and European-Americans; and Christians and non-Christians.

She values diversity and the strength that comes from different perspectives and experiences.

Carol's approach to design requires local knowledge that can best be achieved through partnership. Beginning with the design of

the people's architect **carol ross barney**

the Oklahoma City Federal Building in 1997, her team's inclusion process has been honed over the years to include best practices and tools for engagement.

During recent work for the Invest SW Program in Chicago's Auburn Gresham neighborhood, Ross Barney Architects designed an in-depth engagement process to envision the future of the 79th Street Corridor. Over the course of six weeks, hundreds of residents engaged in a series of open houses and workshops. The conversations informed the design of two buildings.

above Photo of public lecture, courtesy of Ross Barney Architects
below left and right Photos of community engagement. Right photo by Kate Joyce Studios.

From public forums with government and non-profit representatives, to individual conversations with business owners and residents, to multi-day public workshops, design for housing in this dis-invested neighborhood reflects and distills the wishes of the larger community.

19   The Future of Cities

Commodore John Barry Elementary School.
Photo by Matt Wargo Photography.

50 Years of Design Excellence in the Public Realm

Selected Works

24 Designing Democracy
26 Chicago Riverwalk
38 Oklahoma City Federal Building
46 Lincoln Park Zoo Searle Visitor Center
60 NASA Glenn Research Center
Aerospace Communications Facility

74 Infrastructure of Hope
76 Railyard Park
92 CTA Morgan Street Station
102 CTA Cermak/McCormick Place Station
112 O'Hare International Airport
Multi Modal Terminal
128 The Ohio State University
South Campus Chiller Plant

136 Repairing the World
138 Jewish Reconstructionist
Congregation Synagogue
148 UMD Swenson Civil Engineering Building
158 McDonald's Chicago Flagship
172 McDonald's Global Flagship
at Walt Disney World

Designing Democracy

Carol believes that **excellent design is a human right.** Architecture must be **welcoming and inclusive; inviting all** community members to come together. **Good design is democratic**, protecting and creating healthy and sustainable environments for the earth's people.

"Carol's architecture rises directly out of the needs and aspirations of the people who use it ... Over a remarkable career she never quite loses the voice of the people. With little ego and tremendous grit, she is remaking the public sphere in ways that preserve democracy and distribute benefits fairly."

Avinash Rajagopal — Editor-in-Chief, Metropolis Magazine

025

Chicago Riverwalk

Chicago, Illinois

Description Utilizing derelict infrastructure, the Chicago Riverwalk is a one-and-a-quarter-mile-long civic space between Lake Michigan and the confluence of the main, north, and south branches of the Chicago River.

Realizing a vision crafted by Daniel Burnham over a century ago, the park returns Chicago to its river, molding new perceptions, relationships, and an attention to resilience in an ever changing climate.

The park references the infrastructure that defines it by creating unique rooms between the bridges. These new connections enrich and diversify life along the water with each block taking on a unique character and typology.

The river has become the city's living room; an urban counterpoint to Chicago's front yard, Lake Michigan. With a wine bar, kayak tours, boat docking services, water taxi stop, veterans memorial and a myriad of public programs, the city's newest civic space has been mobilized with unthinkable energy.

Collaborative Partners Collins Engineers, Sasaki, Benesch, Jacobs/Ryan Associates, Conservation Design Forum, David Solzman, Delta Engineering Group, Schuler Shook

Size 1.25 miles

Completion Phase I, 2005 & 2009. Phase II, 2015. Phase III, 2016.

Client Chicago Department of Transportation

Selected Recognition AIA Institute Honor Award for Regional & Urban Design, 2018.
AIA Institute Honor Award for Architecture, 2018.
ULI Global Award for Excellence, 2018.
ASLA Honor Award, 2018.
Rudy Bruner Award for Urban Excellence - Silver Medal, 2017.
The Architect's Newspaper Best of Design Award - Urban Design, 2016.
AIA Chicago Distinguished Building, 2016 + 2010.
AIA Illinois Daniel Burnham Honor Award, 2007.
ILASLA Honor Award, 2007.

"The regeneration of the Chicago Riverwalk shows how it is possible to transform former industrial land into a brand new part of the city…"

Sadiq Khan — Mayor of London

Before

Designing Democracy   Selected Work — Chicago Riverwalk

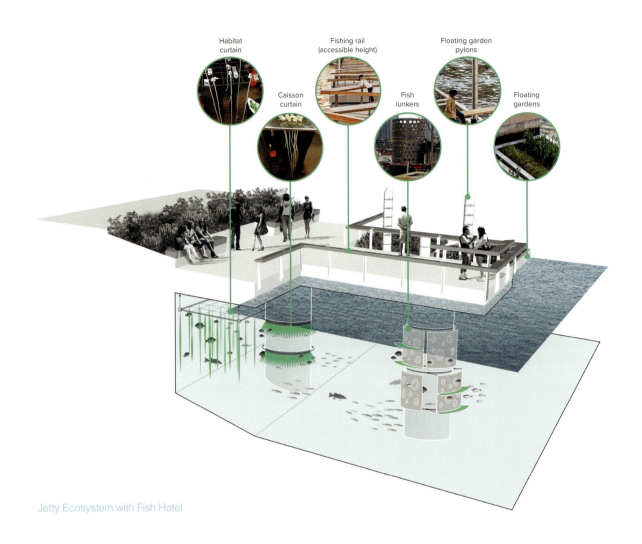

Jetty Ecosystem with Fish Hotel

Under construction

the people's architect **carol ross barney**

Resiliently designed to flood during heavy rain events

100+ native or adapted species thrive at the water's edge

Re-introducing ecology to the main branch of the River

Phase 01 has influenced billions of dollars of development along the Main Branch of the Chicago River

Water quality continues to improve as Chicagoans rediscover this natural asset

Designing Democracy — Selected Work — Chicago Riverwalk

the people's architect **carol ross barney**

The Chicago Riverwalk "may be the most viscerally satisfying new project of the season. We see collections of tall buildings, the streets between them, and people, all presented episodically and in high relief. We are in a living museum - one with no roof and no limits."

Reed Kroloff — *The New York Times*

Designing Democracy · Selected Work — Chicago Riverwalk

Oklahoma City Federal Building

Oklahoma City, Oklahoma

Description In the face of tragedy rises a celebration of democracy that healed a nation. The Oklahoma City Federal Building is a philosophical and practical response to tragedy, making a statement about the role architecture plays in protecting and inspiring society.

An intensive public process included input from survivors, special interest groups and the citizenry in general. The discussions produced important consensus on design goals and suggested solutions to paradoxical requirements; to keep parking away from the building, but provide convenient parking.

The urban-sensitive design integrates security measures while respecting the city, street, and pedestrian. Far from being an impenetrable fortress, the three-story structure embraces an adjacent tree-lined park spread across a city block. At its heart, a glassy elliptical courtyard curves inward to welcome the public and promote a sense of openness.

An enhanced material research process yielded solutions to satisfy blast resistance requirements. "Oklahoma-crete" a colorful and tactile concrete using local stone was developed for a building and site wall that dramatically transforms from landscape partition to a surface that spans the 3 story atrium. An economical and innovative structural glazing method allowed increased glazing while accomplishing the requisite blast protection.

The design results were validated when survivors of the Murrah bombing were able to move back to an open and friendly building with a sense of safety.

Collaborative Partners The Benham Group, Sasaki Associates, Schiff & Associates, Weidlinger Associates, Heery International

Size 185,000 sqft

Completion 2005

Client General Services Administration

Selected Recognition General Services Administration, Design Award, 2006.
AIA Chicago Interior Architecture Award, 2005.
AIA Chicago Divine Detail Award, 2005.
AIA Chicago Sustainable Design Award, 2004.

the people's architect **carol ross barney**

the people's architect carol ross barney

"I think Carol Ross Barney has done a wonderful job. The building is a public place. The federal government is not interested in barricading itself in a bunker, but in fact, make a statement to the public that they own this building, which is what public architecture should be."

Paul Goldberger — ABC Nightline, 2001

Designing Democracy — Selected Work — Oklahoma City Federal Building

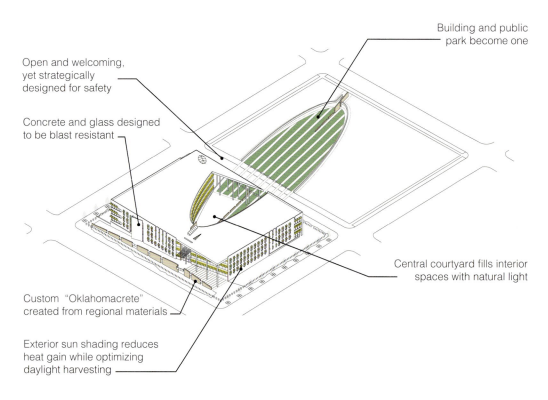

Open and welcoming, yet strategically designed for safety

Concrete and glass designed to be blast resistant

Custom "Oklahomacrete" created from regional materials

Exterior sun shading reduces heat gain while optimizing daylight harvesting

Building and public park become one

Central courtyard fills interior spaces with natural light

the people's architect carol ross barney

Lincoln Park Zoo Searle Visitor Center

Chicago, Illinois

Description The Lincoln Park Zoo, one of North America's oldest, has evolved since its 1868 founding into an institution that connects people with nature in the heart of Chicago.

The new pavilion, which comprises an entry gate, visitors center, administrative offices, membership lounge, and public washrooms, tucks behind a natural landscape. Two buildings formed in the shape of a "J" are visually tied together by an innovative structural canopy. Cantilevered frames support and hang from one another. These opposing forces: tension and compression, balance out in an effect that appears to effortlessly levitate. As visitors gaze up, a pattern of layered branches filters light as if peering through the canopy of a tree.

Against the backdrop of Lake Michigan (850 ft. away), the building springs to life in warmer months; blurring the definition between interior and exterior. Here, a memorable building serves as a gateway to the zoo, park, city, and world beyond.

Collaborative Partners Goodfriend Magruder, Terra, IMEG, Jacobs Ryan Associates, Bulley & Andrews

Size 9,500 sqft

Completion 2018

Client Lincoln Park Zoo

Selected Recognition International Architecture Award, The Chicago Athenaeum and the European Center for Art and Design, 2021. American Architecture Award, The Chicago Athenaeum, 2020.

LEED Silver Certified

the people's architect **carol ross barney**

Closed Wall

the people's architect **carol ross barney**　　　　　50

Open Wall

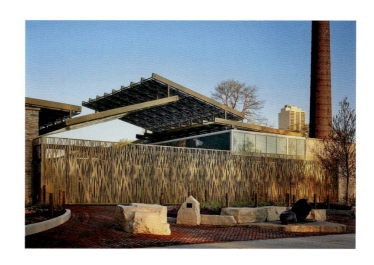

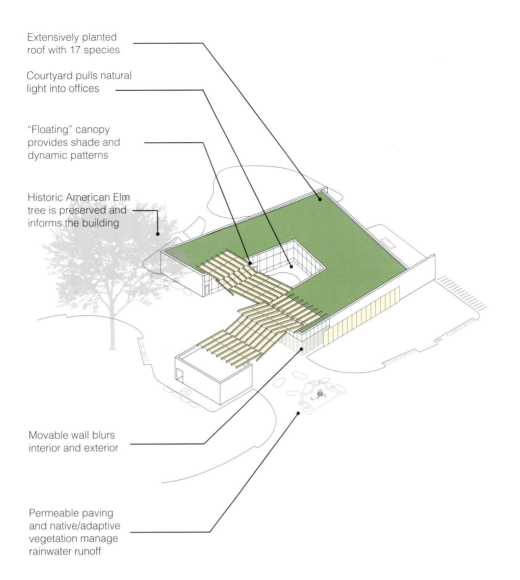

- Extensively planted roof with 17 species
- Courtyard pulls natural light into offices
- "Floating" canopy provides shade and dynamic patterns
- Historic American Elm tree is preserved and informs the building
- Movable wall blurs interior and exterior
- Permeable paving and native/adaptive vegetation manage rainwater runoff

Designing Democracy   55   Selected Work — Lincoln Park Zoo Searle Visitor Center

"The nature-inspired design practices mimesis, the act of representing the natural world in art. The pattern also reflects how zoos increasingly view themselves as oases of nature in an urbanizing world. It reflects the skill of the firm's namesake, Carol Ross Barney, at shaping vibrant public spaces."

Chicago Tribune, Blair Kamin —
Pulitzer Prize Winning Architecture Critic

the people's architect **carol ross barney**

NASA Glenn Research Center Aerospace Communications Facility

Cleveland, Ohio

Description The new 55,000 sf Aerospace Communications Facility (ACF) consolidates research laboratories that were located in seven different buildings on Lewis Field into a single, state of the art research facility consisting of efficient, flexible laboratories, anechoic test chambers, RF-shielded laboratories, collaboration spaces, information technology support areas, and a dedicated rooftop platform for communications antennas.

A prominent feature of the façade is an articulated skin that reflects the pragmatism of the campus. Etched concrete, glass, corrugated metal, and an undulating sunscreen work to broadcast research and create interior environments that foster innovation, create light-filled spaces, and echo the research within.

The building achieved a LEED Gold rating and is designed to be Net Zero Energy Ready (NZER). The design team investigated energy use drivers (including a current plug load survey), established an EUI target, analyzed the building design and systems, performed an energy cost summary, calculated anticipated CO_2 emissions, cataloged life cycle costs, identified return on investments for optimized building systems, and identified the site's potential for renewable energy production.

Collaborative Partners APTIM, dbHMS, Environmental Design Group, Field Management Services Guidepost Solutions, HERA Laboratory Planners, Terracon, The Concord Group, Thornton Tomasetti, Thornton Tomasetti-Weidlinger Protective Design, Threshold Acoustics, Waveguide Consulting

Size 55,500 sqft

Completion 2023

Client NASA Glenn Research Center

LEED Gold Certified; Net Zero Energy Ready

the people's architect **carol ross barney**

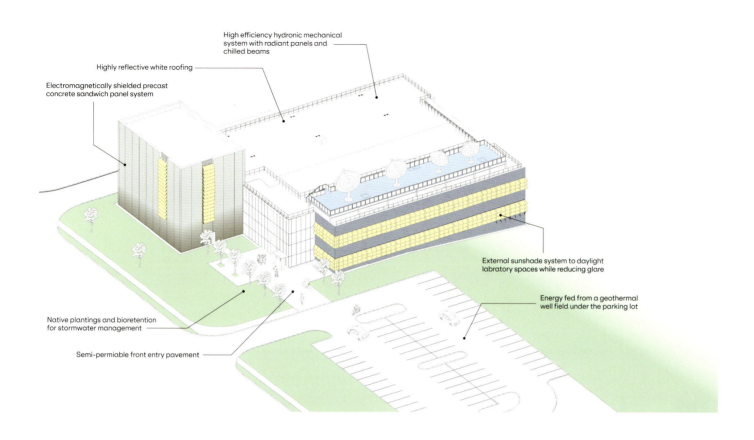

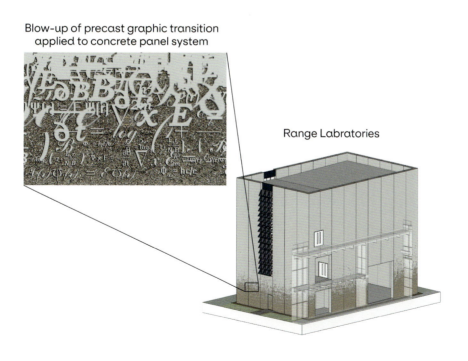

The Near Field Range, an anechoic laboratory for testing antennas and antenna systems, is clad in custom designed etched concrete full of scientific equations. The faded graphic reduces the scale of the 60 foot laboratory, creating a backdrop for the adjacent outdoor amenity space/plaza.

An articulated skin wraps the building's laboratories with a sunscreen that controls daylight. Slight undulations were tested for visual and environmental impact. This included a full scale mock-up by the design team to test the perforated corrugated metal's effectiveness at preserving views while blocking harsh sun and glare.

The anechoic laboratory for testing antennas and antenna systems is located within the 60 ft shielded space for both electromagnetic and radio frequency interference. The lab is located adjacent to an overhead door for ease of moving large scale antennae inside the building.

Designing Democracy   67   Selected Work — NASA ACF

The building program prioritized shared research space and opted to pilot a hoteling work concept over private offices. The resulting lounge and conference space sits adjacent to the ravine, providing a dynamic backdrop year-round.

Designing Democracy 69 Selected Work — NASA ACF

the people's architect **carol ross barney**

Infrastructure of Hope

Typically, **designing infrastructure is not even considered architecture.** Infrastructure plays a vital role in the **connectivity** and **efficiency** of our cities. And its design contributes to the quality of urban life. With a growing portfolio of projects situated on these "fringes of architecture", Carol has continued to tackle increasingly complex cultural, social, and spatial challenges; transforming everyday **moments** into **design opportunities.**

"Someone asked me to describe Carol and I thought; if Robert Moses and Jane Jacobs had a secret love child it would be Carol. You get the combination of big civic aspiration coupled with activated spaces on a human scale."

Mike Waldinger, Hon. AIA — Executive Director, AIA Colorado
Former Executive VP, AIA Illinois

075

Railyard Park

Rogers, Arkansas

Description Rogers as a city has been defined both economically and physically by the St. Louis and San Francisco Railroad. As industry shifted so too did the spaces that facilitated train operation: the depot was demolished and loading/unloading space was no longer needed.

With a grant from the Walton Family Foundation, the City of Rogers embarked on a project to design a new downtown park that would enhance economic development, spur placemaking, and improve connectivity.

The design process for the Railyard used the most expansive community outreach effort in Northwest Arkansas history; developing a shared vision, sense of pride, and park that is distinctly Rogers.

A series of plazas transform throughout the day, week, month, and year. These densely vegetated and programmed spaces create unique experiences throughout the park and further frame this piece of downtown as the new center instead of the edge.

Collaborative Partners Goodfriend Magruder, Schuler Shook, CEI Engineers, HP Engineering, Span, AFHJ Architects, Grubbs Hoskyn Barton + Wyatt

Size 4.6 acres

Completion 2021

Client City of Rogers, Arkansas

Selected Recognition American Institute of Architects, Regional and Urban Design Award, 2023.
Innovation by Design, Fast Company Magazine, 2022.
The Architects Newspaper, Best of Award, Unbuilt, 2020.

the people's architect **carol ross barney**

"Ross Barney Architects met and exceeded our expectations. Their public outreach sessions never felt as if the design team was checking a box: participants felt they were part of the design process itself. It was remarkable, and essential to the public embracing (and enthusiastically using) the park. Railyard Park was immediately and significantly impactful as a direct result of that engagement. We are thrilled with the results!"

John McCurdy, Community Development - Director, City of Rogers, AR.

Engagement Strategy
The project utilized a robust community engagement strategy. Attendees at an initial Open House were asked to identify with a colored dot where they lived, worked, and played. 70% of those who attended lived within a two-mile radius of the park, helping inform the spirit of comments received.

Goals
The park's success is reliant on community stewardship. In that spirit collective goals were refined throughout the engagement process to help evoke the emotional, aesthetic, and programmatic aspirations.

the people's architect carol ross barney

1,043 total responses

75% completion rate (776)

Q1 How often do you visit Downtown Rogers?

- Daily **22%**
- Weekly **39%**
- Monthly **21%**
- A few times a year **17%**
- Never **1%**

Q2 How far do you travel to get to Downtown Rogers?

< 1 mile | 1 mile | 2 miles | 3 miles | < 4 miles

Q3 What mode of transportation do you typically use to get to Downtown Rogers?

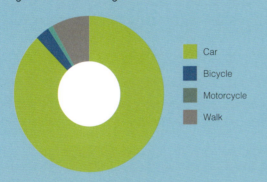

- Car
- Bicycle
- Motorcycle
- Walk

Q4 What best describes your relationship to Downtown Rogers?

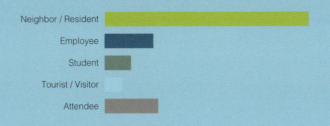

- Neighbor / Resident
- Employee
- Student
- Tourist / Visitor
- Attendee

Q5 What time of day do you typically visit Downtown Rogers?

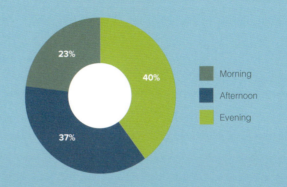

- Morning **23%**
- Afternoon **37%**
- Evening **40%**

Q6 Do you come Downtown alone or w/ others (in general)?

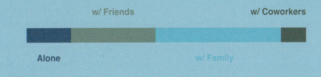

Alone | w/ Friends | w/ Family | w/ Coworkers

Q7 What is the primary reason for your visit to Downtown Rogers?

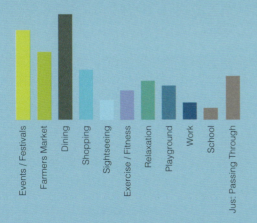

Events / Festivals, Farmers Market, Dining, Shopping, Sightseeing, Exercise / Fitness, Relaxation, Playground, Work, School, Just Passing Through

Q8 What three words would you use to describe Downtown Rogers?

Beautiful, Unique, Historic, Fun, Food, Relaxed, Charming, Quaint, Eclectic, Hometown, Potential

Engagement Tools

The methods used for engagement were both physical and digital, providing formats of contribution that were comfortable and meaningful. The results yielded 20,000+ data points that informed the design.

1 Frisco Plaza
2 Regional Bike Trails
3 Event Building
4 Butterfield Stage
5 Pop-up Plaza
6 Playard
7 Water Stop
8 Railroad Tracks

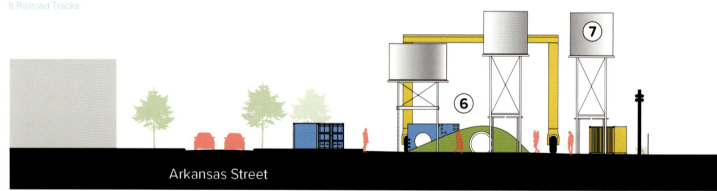

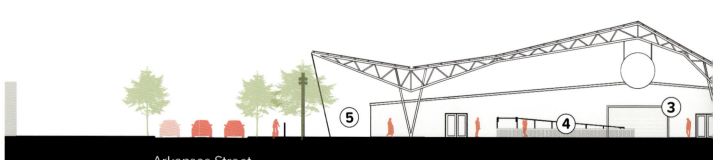

the people's architect carol ross barney   82

"Many designers would find an active railway an impediment to the creation of a new five-acre public park. The Arkansas & Missouri Railroad train tracks that run through downtown Rogers, Arkansas, were a local trademark worth venerating, not obscuring. Ross Barney Architect's design for the new track-straddling Railyard Park embraces its industrial heritage while transforming it into a vibrant outdoor destination for the community."

The Architect's Newspaper - Matt Hickman

Infrastructure of Hope — Selected Work — Railyard Park

- Walnut Street Historic District
- Active Rail Line
- Economic development opportunities east of rail line
- Existing Tyson facility
- Recreational assets

"Elevating the design of Northwest Arkansas's public spaces isn't just a tourism play," says Karen Minkel, Walton Family Foundation Program Director. "We have a vision for this region to be one of the most vibrant and inclusive communities in the country," she adds. "When you have groups of people who have different perspectives and experiences gathered in one space, design becomes a tool for inclusion."

Metropolis Magazine - Addie Broyles

the people's architect carol ross barney

Infrastructure of Hope   87   Selected Work — Railyard Park

CTA Green Line Infill Stations

CTA Morgan Street Station

Aging infrastructure is America's next greatest challenge. Two stations on the Chicago Transit Authority's Green Line are strong testaments to the value design excellence has in everyday life. The attention to detail, context, and overall experience elevates a daily task into a celebrated moment of travel and excitement.

Emblematic of their neighborhoods, these stations assert themselves as part of a larger context and are a strong testament to the evolving modernity of Chicago's mass transit system.

CTA Cermak-McCormick Place Station

CTA
Morgan Street Station

Chicago, Illinois

Description
Set against the scenery of Chicago's West Loop, formerly a warehouse district full of meat packers, the station pays homage to an industrial past with an exposed structure, perforated metal, and tough finishes. These materials hold up against the unforgiving context without compromising a sense of celebration and inspiration.

Confined by a narrow right-of-way, the station exploits its constraints by accommodating necessary at-grade functions into an area equal to three parallel parking spaces. As the extruded plan rises, the platform and bridge connecting inbound and outbound service weaves through and above the existing structure.

Morgan Street Station became the first new project to join the CTA system in over twenty years and showed a city that transit can look contemporary, bold, beautiful, and, most importantly, maintainable; resulting in an increased standard of design quality. With over one-million annual riders, the station has influenced development and encouraged a corporate resurgence Downtown that values urban connectivity.

Collaborative Partners
TranSystems, LTK Engineering Services, OSA Engineers, H.W. Lochner, Muller+Muller, F.H. Paschen, S.N. Nielsen, Arup

Size
2 - 480 ft. platforms, 2 station houses at grade

Completion
2012

Client
Chicago Department of Transportation and Chicago Transit Authority

Selected Recognition
ULI Chicago Vision Award, 2015.
AIA Chicago Divine Detail, 2013.
World Architecture Festival High Commendation, Transport, 2013.
Friends of Downtown Best of Downtown Award, 2013.
Chicago Architecture Patron of the Year, 2012.
AIA Chicago Distinguished Building, 2012.

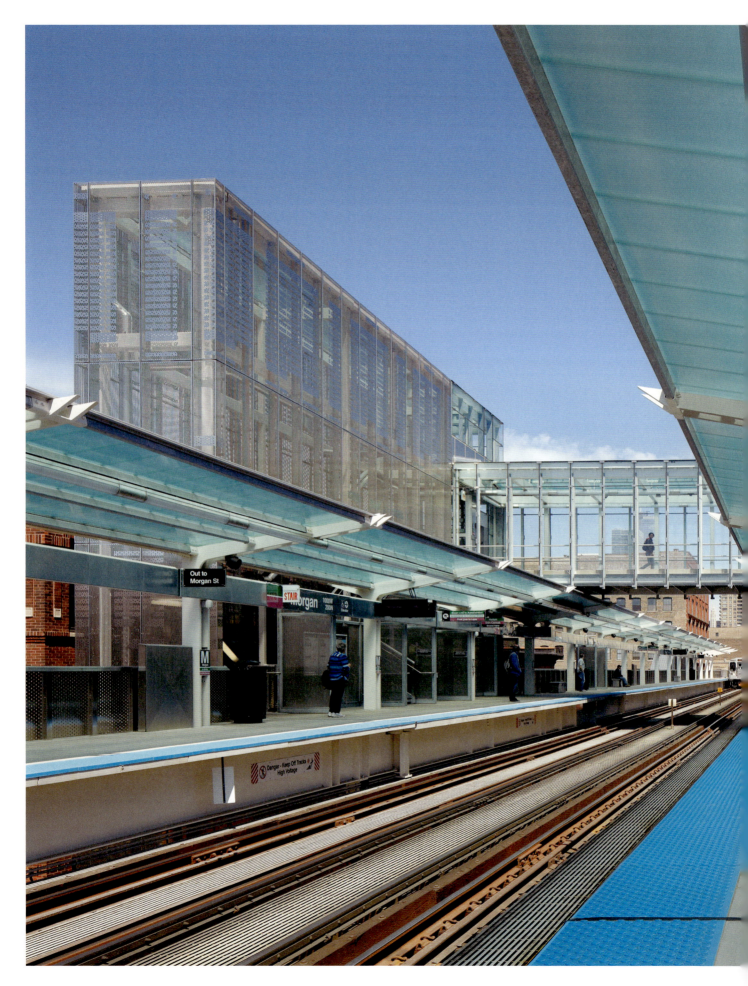

2012

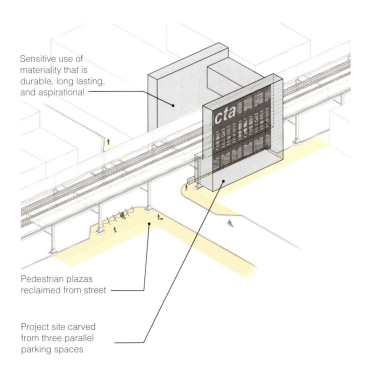

Sensitive use of materiality that is durable, long lasting, and aspirational

Pedestrian plazas reclaimed from street

Project site carved from three parallel parking spaces

the people's architect **carol ross barney**

"The fabulous new CTA Morgan Street station was a factor in our decision to re-locate employees to the Fulton Market District."

Google Chicago, Jim Lecinski

"The station's spectral stair towers and glass-sheathed transfer bridge rise airily above the hard-edged warehouses and cold meat lockers of the West Loop, also home to trendy restaurants and galleries. The area, it's been said, is in transition from slaughterhouses to art houses. The Oprah show may be gone, but the station is a new jewel in the West Loop's crown."

Chicago Tribune - Blair Kamin - Pulitzer Prize Winning Architecture Critic

the people's architect **carol ross barney**

CTA Cermak/McCormick Place Station

Chicago, Illinois

Description Like many infill projects along the Chicago Transit system, a narrow right-of-way creates challenges for building out a system to better serve diverse communities. Utilizing constraints as an opportunity, the station takes the form of a tube; creating efficiency for platform function and structure.

Clad in perforated stainless steel, the skin provides protection to patrons while preserving views and a feeling of openness. Three perforated panel patterns were used to reduce wind penetration, maintain visibility, and maximize views without compromising natural light. The convergence of these approaches yields a subtle pattern that allows the station to breath on a hot summer day and protect riders from harsh winter winds.

The station has helped generate billions of dollars in development and sits at the center of a burgeoning entertainment district. With a new events arena, convention center expansion, hotels, retail, and residential, Cermak Mc-Cormick Place serves over a half-million passengers a year; providing surprise and delight to a utilitarian experience.

Collaborative Partners T.Y. Lin International, Singh & Associates, OSA Engineers, H.W. Lochner, Muller+Muller, F.H. Paschen, S.N. Nielsen, Arup

Size 1-480 Ft Platform, Station Houses at Grade

Completion 2016

Client Chicago Department of Transportation and Chicago Transit Authority

Selected Recognition AIA Illinois Mies Van der Rohe Award, 2018
AIA, Chicago Distinguished Building, 2015.
World Architecture Festival Transport, 2016.
AIA, Chicago Divine Detail, 2015.
American Public Works Association,
Chicago Project of the Year, 2016.

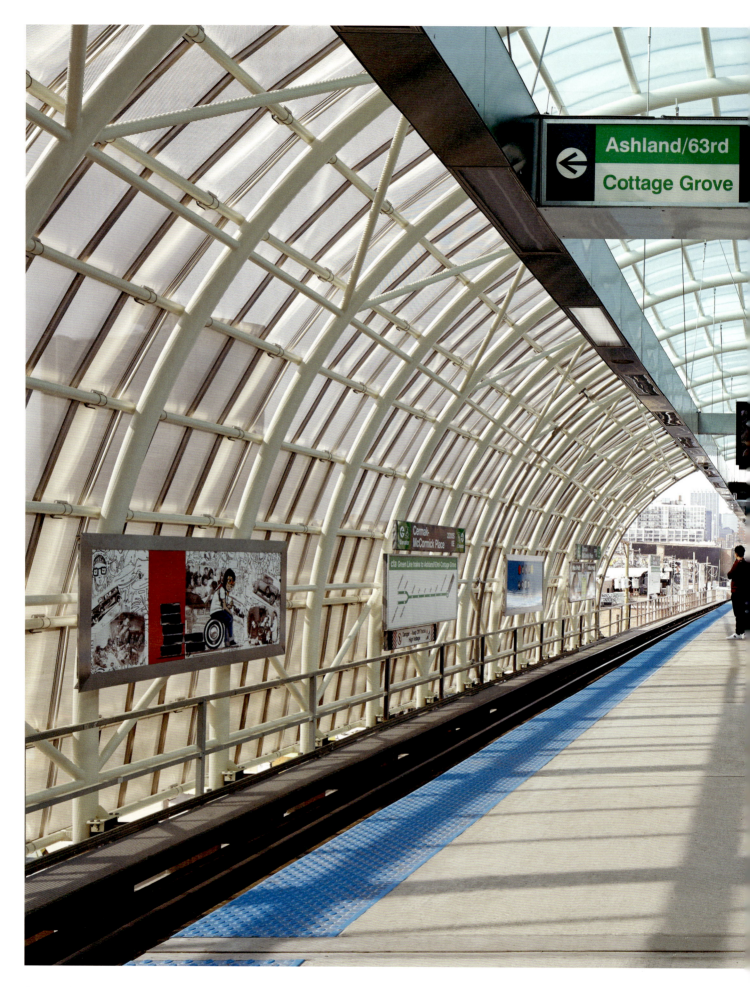

the people's architect **carol ross barney**

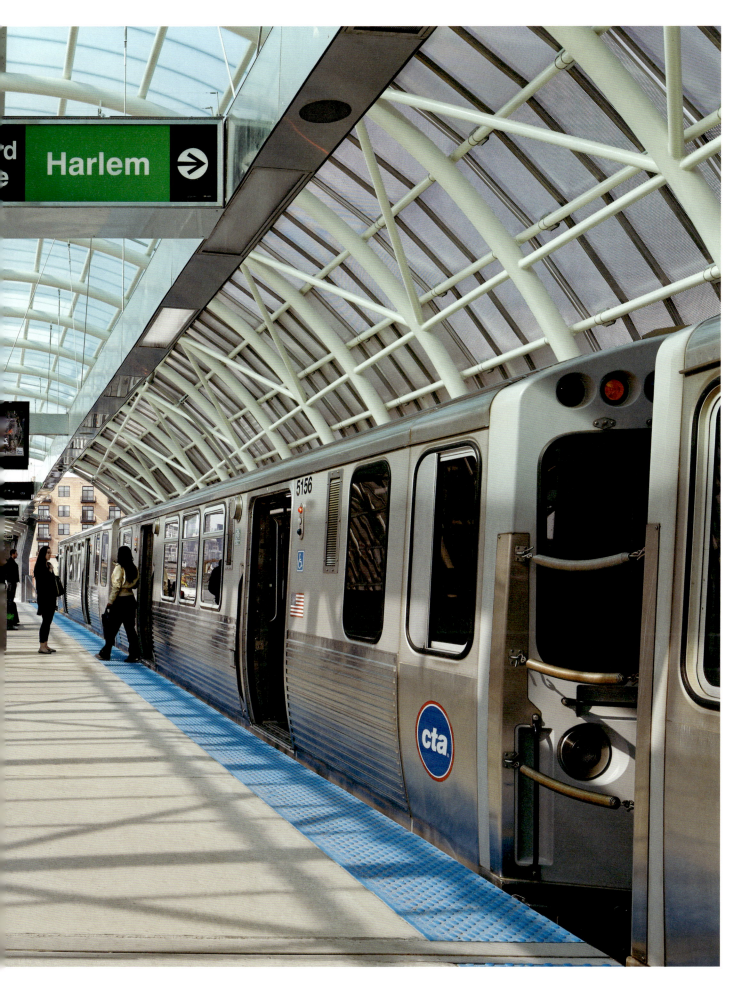

Infrastructure of Hope — Selected Work — CTA Cermak/McCormick Place Station

"The new station makes a civic statement. There's no clutter, just an airy, column free space. From within, travelers can look through the tube's perforated metal skin and see McCormick Place, orienting themselves."

Chicago Tribune - Blair Kamin - Pulitzer Prize Winning Architecture Critic

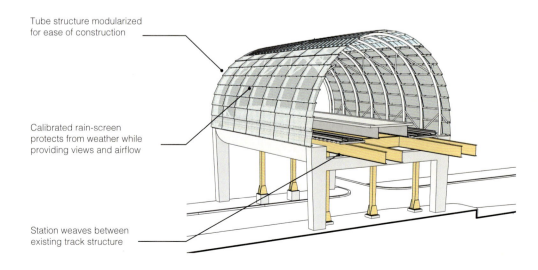

Tube structure modularized for ease of construction

Calibrated rain-screen protects from weather while providing views and airflow

Station weaves between existing track structure

the people's architect **carol ross barney**

"Ross Barney Architects' long-standing relationship with the Chicago Transit Authority has delivered the system's best contemporary stations and renovations."

Metropolis Magazine - Zach Mortice

 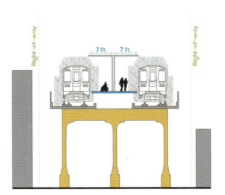 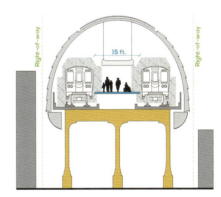

Canopy Design Evolution

Infrastructure of Hope · Selected Work — CTA Cermak/McCormick Place Station

the people's architect **carol ross barney**

O'Hare International Airport Multi Modal Terminal

Chicago, Illinois

Description The new 3 million square feet Multi-Modal Terminal at O'Hare International Airport connects the airport's ground transportation options in one spot with a 1.5 mile extension of the Airport Transit System, or People Mover. This welcoming and convenient gateway to Chicago is a soaring, sun filled terminal serving the customers of rental car companies, regional buses and trains and hotel shuttles.

A major influence on the design is CDA's "Sustainable Airport Manual", goals of which are to demonstrate Chicago's commitment to sustainable construction and to use facilities to teach about sustainable building practices. The building received LEED Silver certification and its sustainable features include; expansive planted green walls, 22% energy cost savings through whole building energy simulation, salvaged, recycled and re-used materials on site, FSC certified wood and 99% of overall waste diverted from landfills.

The City of Chicago commissioned original art curated by Theaster Gates and includes "Horizon Light" by James Carpenter, "Field Lines" by Rob Ley, "Palimpsest" by Nick Cave and "Reach" by Hank Willis Thomas and Coby Kennedy.

Collaborative Partners TranSystems, Delta Engineering, Singh & Associates, Walker Parking, Austin Power Partners

Size 3,000,000 sf

Completion 2019

Client Chicago Department of Aviation

Selected Recognition AIA Chicago Design Excellence Awards, Architecture XL, 2023.
International CODAward, Collaboration of Design and Art, 2021.

LEED Silver Certified
3 Green Airplane Designation, Sustainable Airport Manual

the people's architect **carol ross barney**

the people's architect carol ross barney

"Horizon Light" Art Work by James Carpenter

the people's architect **carol ross barney**

"Field Lines" artwork by Rob Ley
Photos on this page by Alan Tansey

the people's architect **carol ross barney**

"Palimpsest" Art Work by Nick Cave

"Reach" artwork by Hank Willis Thomas and Coby Kennedy

Infrastructure of Hope 121 Selected Work — O'Hare International Airport Multi Modal Terminal

"Field Lines" artwork by Rob Ley
Photo by Alan Tansey

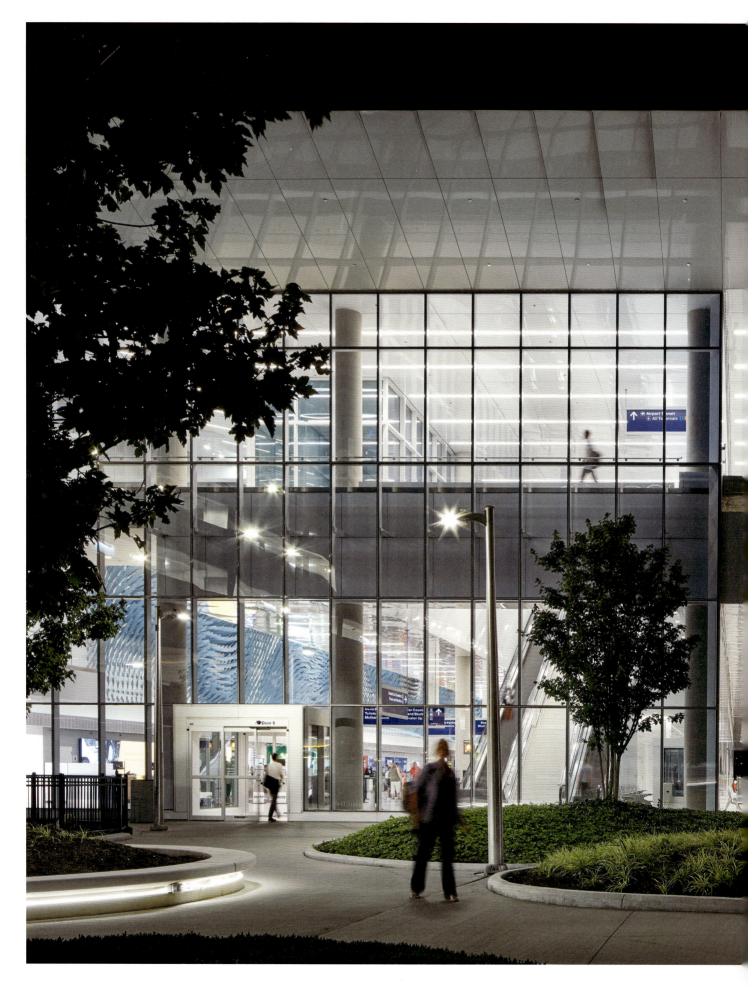

the people's architect carol ross barney

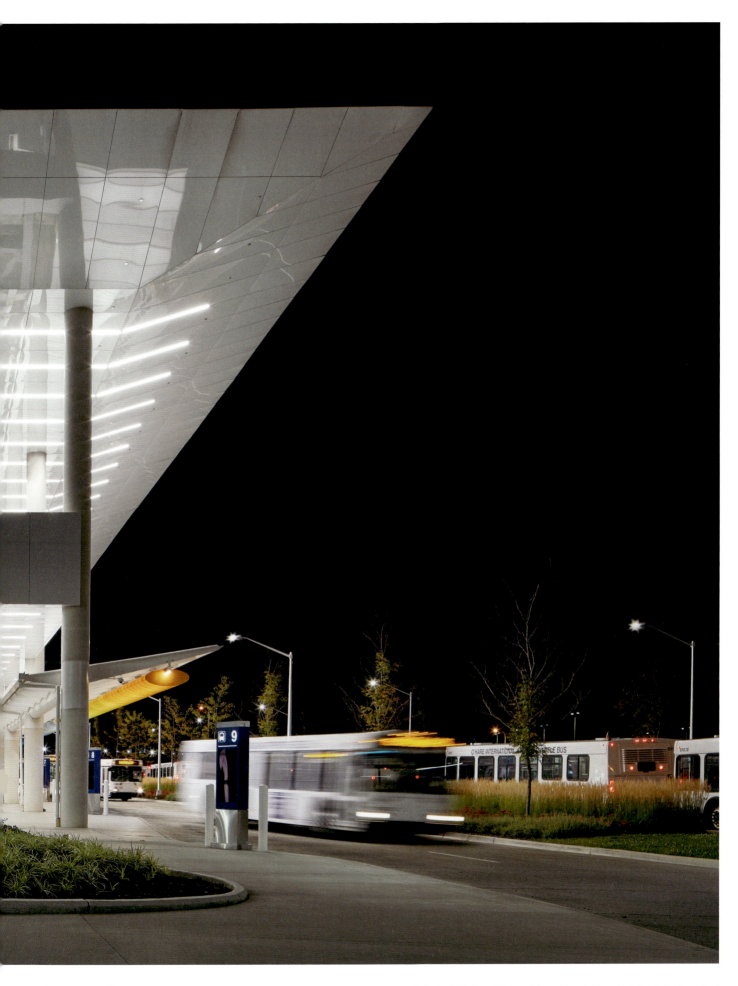

The Ohio State University South Campus Chiller Plant

Columbus, Ohio

Description	Utilitarian in function, this collegiate infrastructure building has no active users. Often a campus backdrop or seen as an active eyesore, how do you make a house for energy an icon?

The response to this challenge is a technical façade composed of precast concrete panels that preserves views of the equipment. Seemingly random at first glance, the ordered façade of two-hundred panels is based on repetition, efficiency, and function; utilizing just nineteen panel types.

Working in collaboration with a glass manufacturer, the design team created the first exterior use of dichroic film, a metallic inner layer that alters the wavelength and therefore the color of light passing through. The result is a dynamic showcase that changes with the time of day, season, and location of the observer. |
Collaborative Partners	Champlin Architects, Lupton/Rausch Architects, Whiting-Turner, RMF Engineering, Shelley Metz Baumann Hawk, Jones Stuckey, MSI Design, Arup
Size	95,737 sqft
Completion	2013
Client	Ohio State University
Selected Recognition	Architizer A+ Awards, 2017.
AIA Chicago Divine Detail, 2017.
AIA Chicago Distinguished Building, 2014.
World Architecture News Color in Architecture Finalist, 2014.
Prestressed Concrete Institution Award, 2014.

LEED Silver Certified

the people's architect **carol ross barney**

Infrastructure of Hope　　　131　Selected Work — The Ohio State University South Campus Chiller Plant

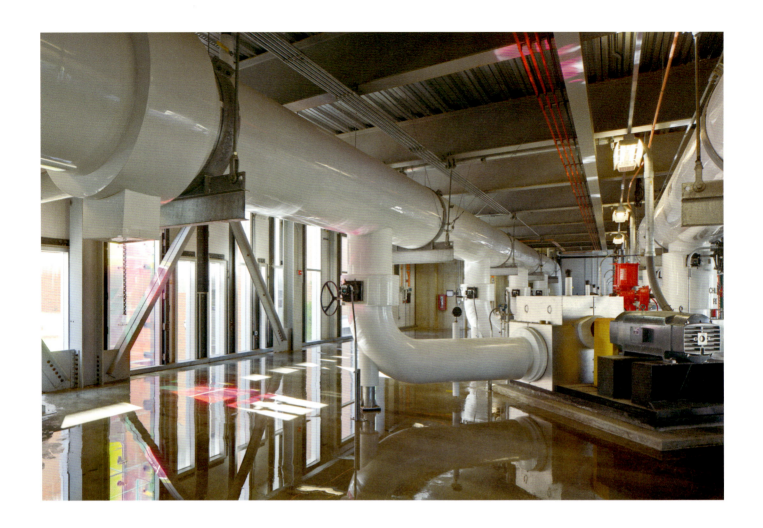

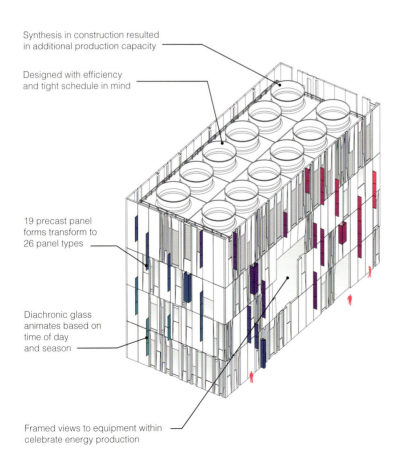

Synthesis in construction resulted in additional production capacity

Designed with efficiency and tight schedule in mind

19 precast panel forms transform to 26 panel types

Diachronic glass animates based on time of day and season

Framed views to equipment within celebrate energy production

the people's architect **carol ross barney**

Repairing the World

Carol's embrace of sustainability is inspired by her service with the **U.S. Peace Corps for the National Parks of Costa Rica** where she worked on the restoration of natural ecologies. She has produced a remarkable succession of projects at all scales and uses. Whether or not it received a LEED certification, **each project embeds sustainable principles**. This reflects her ethical belief that a project should **improve the world and teach the community** about environmental stewardship.

"Most architects dream of making the world a better place. Carol actually gets it done."

Reed Kroloff, Dean, IIT College of Architecture and Former Editor, *Architect Magazine*

137

Jewish Reconstructionist Congregation Synagogue

Evanston, Illinois

Description Tikkun Olam, a Jewish concept defined by acts of kindness to repair the world manifests itself through an assertive use of sustainable and ethical architecture.

The Jewish Reconstructionist Congregation became the world's first LEED Platinum house of worship and balances an ambitious program, sustainable rigor, and small site while maintaining a modest budget.

The response is a holistic approach to aesthetics, materials, and nature. Exterior wood cladding was recycled from demolished barns while the ceremonial door is composed from trees removed from the site during construction, paying homage to the congregation's history. The existing building's foundations and demolition spoils make up a perimeter gabion wall that frames the site.

Offices, classrooms, and adaptable community spaces occupy the lower levels while the sanctuary, accessed by a processional stair, sits atop the tree canopy. Throughout the year, nature affords congregants a sublime backdrop for worship, fellowship, and community.

Collaborative Partners C.E. Anderson & Associates, EYP Mission Critical Facilities, Talaske, Cotter Consulting, Bulley & Andrews

Size 31,000 sqft

Completion 2008

Client Jewish Reconstructionist Congregation Synagogue

Selected Recognition AIA COTE Top Ten Award, 2009.
Design Evanston Award, 2010.
World Architecture Festival High,
Commendation Community Buildings, 2009.
AIA Illinois Honor Award, 2008.

LEED Platinum Certified

Repairing the World 141 Selected Work — Jewish Reconstructionist Congregation Synagogue

Sustainable Strategies
1 Reflective roof mitigates heat island effect and keeps building cooler.
2 Stormwater detention system eases the impact of storm water on the environment and municipal system.
3 Landscaped with native and adapted plants, included transplants from the original landscaping. No permanent irrigation used for landscaping.
4 Exterior light fixtures have full cut-off optics to mitigate light pollution.
5 Access to daylight and views for over 90% of the spaces.
6 Operable windows in all the spaces for option of natural ventilation.
7 Spectrally selective and low emissivity glazing used to reduce heat load and harmful UV rays.
8 Ceremonial door cladding milled from on-site crimson maple trees that were displaced due to new construction.
9 Reclaimed wood from mushroom houses used for exterior siding.
10 Gabion site walls made from locally demolished brick, concrete, and limestone.

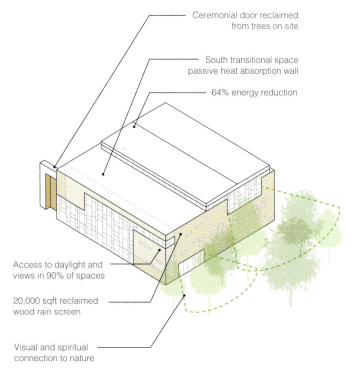

"The JRC Board resolved to build a new synagogue that would be as green as feasible ... that led to the first LEED Platinum place of worship in the world. Underlying the congregation's resolve were Bal Tashchit, which teaches 'do not destroy or waste' as well as ... Tikun Olam, 'repairing the world' ... In Ross Barney Architects, the congregation found a partner who shared their commitment. We have learned that it is not the building but the process of building that creates sacred community."
- Rabbi Brant Rosen, client.

Design for Re-Use Primer, Version 2.0 - Public Architecture - *The Architectural Review* - Mimi Zeiger

the people's architect **carol ross barney**

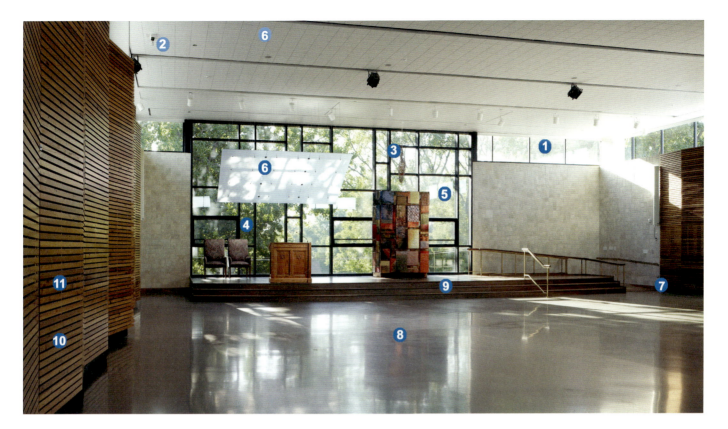

Sustainable Strategies
1 Access to daylight and views for over 90% of the spaces.
2 Dimming and photocell controls for maximizing daylighting.
3 Eternal light is solar powered.
4 Operable windows in all spaces for option of natural ventilation.
5 Spectrally selective and low emissivity glazing used to reduce heat load and harmful UV rays.
6 Sound baffle and ceiling tiles made from recycled materials.
7 Low VOC emitting materials.
8 Polished concrete floor eliminates need for floor covering material, while providing a beautiful, low-maintenance and durable floor. Concrete uses recycled fly-ash in mix.
9 Bimah flooring milled from downed Chicago Park District black walnut trees.
10 Displacement ventilation system used in Sanctuary.
11 Reclaimed wood from mushroom houses used for interior slat walls. Slat walls serve to hide ventilation system, while providing acoustical paneling.

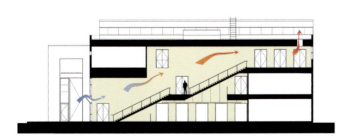
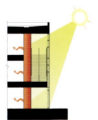
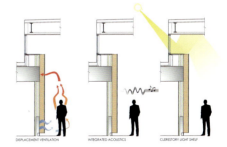

South Stair Transitional Space   **Sanctuary Slat Wall Sections**

Repairing the World   143   Selected Work — Jewish Reconstructionist Congregation Synagogue

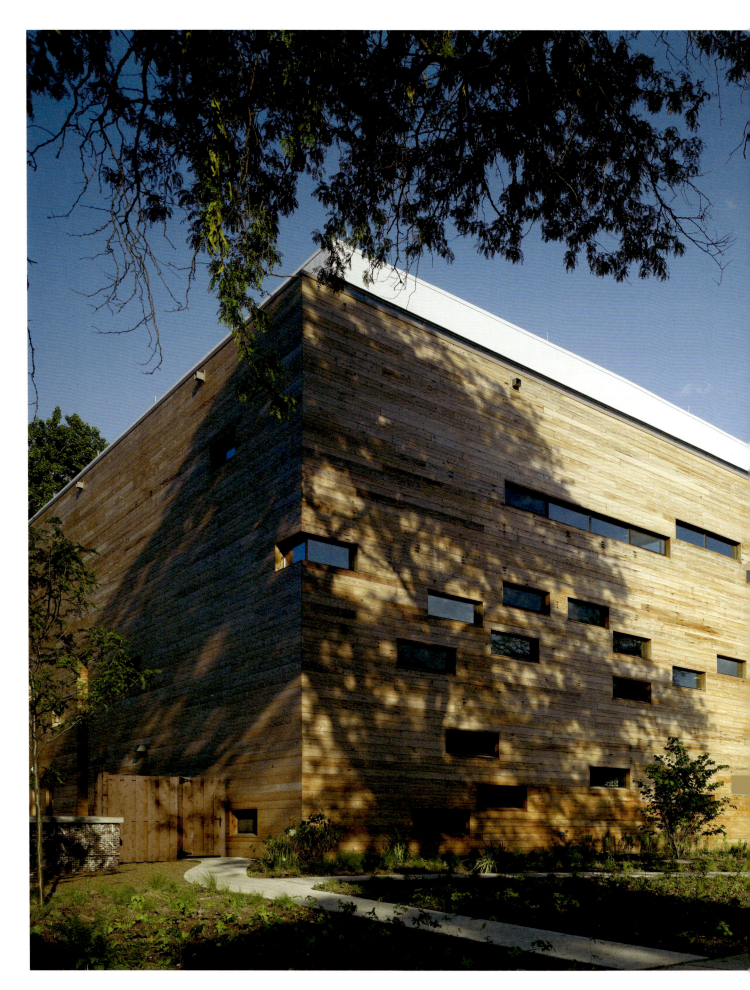

the people's architect carol ross barney

"It is one thing to be virtuous and another thing to be beautiful. And the synagogue turns out to be better at blending these two. This is an inspiring space, fit for 21st Century worship, where the aesthetic and the environmental are perfectly in sync."

Chicago Tribune - Blair Kamin - Pulitzer Prize Winning Architecture Critic

UMD Swenson Civil Engineering Building

Duluth, Minnesota

Description We started by asking, "What do engineers need to learn, and what forces do they need to control?" In that pedagogical spirit, the new 35,300-square-foot building for civil engineering at the University of Minnesota Duluth is designed to teach students about materials, how they go together, how they age, and how they resist the forces inherent in nature.

The exterior uses rusting steel, precast and poured-in-place concrete and reclaimed wood to create a place for designing, constructing, and testing structure. Taconite, abundant nearby, fills drums that collect stormwater for experimentation in laboratory flumes. Excess rainwater is carried by taconite rock drains to onsite retention, or is absorbed by the vegetated roof.

The wood scuppers made from recycled pickle barrels teach use of salvaged materials in a new building. (And add the scent of pickles under certain conditions.) On rainy days, the building demonstrates hydraulic and kinetic energy, as water pours from the scuppers.

The civil engineering department saw this building as a recruiting tool, and the design supports that mission. What aspiring civil engineer can resist a building that spouts water, corrodes constructively before your very eyes — and has the biggest toys on campus?

Collaborative Partners Stanius Johnson Architects, Stahl Construction, MBJ Consulting, Dunham Engineering, MSA Professional Services, Inc., Oslund and Associates

Size 35,000 sqft

Completion 2010

Client University of Minnesota Duluth

Selected Recognition AIA COTE Top Ten Award, 2013.
AIA Committee on Architecture for Education, Award of Merit, 2013.
AIA Chicago SustainABILITY, 2013.
The Chicago Athenaeum American Architecture Award, 2012.
AIA Chicago Distinguished Building, 2011.

LEED Gold Certified

the people's architect **carol ross barney**

the people's architect carol ross barney

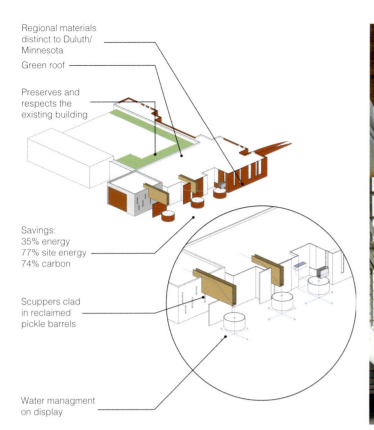

Regional materials distinct to Duluth/Minnesota

Green roof

Preserves and respects the existing building

Savings:
35% energy
77% site energy
74% carbon

Scuppers clad in reclaimed pickle barrels

Water managment on display

Repairing the World — 153 — Selected Work — UMD Swenson Civil Engineering Building

Teaching continues inside with exposed mechanical and architectural systems. Structural glass partitions and clerestories allow daylighting and views to the laboratories.

Sustainable highlights include: stormwater management, 30% recycled content building materials, 20% locally sourced materials, displacement air distribution keeping the 30-foot high labs comfortable without conditioning total air volume, and a 56% reduction in the use of potable water through recycling and conservation.

McDonald's Flagship Restaurants

McDonald's Global Flagship at Walt Disney World Resort

Buildings are responsible for approximately 40% of global CO2 emissions. McDonald's has committed to evolve its 2030 goals to put them on the pathway toward achieving net zero emission across their global operations by 2050.

McDonald's utilizes a multi-pronged approach in reducing environmental impact through its "Scale for Good" strategy (Food Quality and Sourcing, Packaging, Water Stewardship, Food Waste, Real Estate Impact, and a focus on employee health and well being). Both Flagship restaurants in Chicago and Walt Disney World are a continuation of this strategy, using architecture and technology to embody impactful symbols of change.

No one building or building type will solve the climate crisis. Quick service restaurants are dependent on an automobile-centric culture that is not likely to change for the foreseeable future. In the past few years McDonald's has explored how to evolve this often overlooked building type in climate conversations as a design and environmental storyteller. The flagships in Chicago and at Walt Disney World may seem contradictory at first glance but represent significant thought, strategy, and investment in testing scalable technologies.

McDonald's Chicago Flagship

McDonald's Chicago Flagship

Chicago, Illinois

Description McDonald's Chicago flagship radically deviates from a typical prototype restaurant. The building begins to ask new questions about customer experience and impact. While one-of-a-kind, the flagship is generating valuable lessons that can be scaled to an expansive portfolio—impacting communities around the world.

A solar pergola unites the restaurant while also providing 55% of electrical energy needs (2020 production was above projections). Beneath this "big roof," indoor dining areas seamlessly connect to permeable outdoor plazas and a park.

In the dining room, Cross Laminated Timber (CLT) and Glulam beams are celebrated against a backdrop of white birch trees planted in a suspended atrium and hanging "plant tapestries." The restaurant is the first commercial project in Chicago to use CLT.

The flagship is a case study in environmental stewardship, embodying a global brand's commitment to action all while creating a city oasis where people can eat, drink, and meet.

Collaborative Partners Landini Associates, Goodfriend Magruder Structures, Omni Ecosystems, WCW Engineers, Dickerson Electrical Engineers, Schuler Shook, Day and Night Solar, Watermark Engineering, Compass Surveying, Sevan Solutions

Size 19,065 sqft

Completion 2018

Client McDonald's Corporation

Selected Recognition Architizer A+Awards, 2022.
Planet Positive Award, Metropolis Magazine, 2021.
International Architecture Award, Chicago Athenaeum/European Center for Design, 2020.
1st Prize - Sustainability Award, Archmarathon, 2020.
Limelight Award, Illinois Green Alliance, 2019.
North America Special Prize, Prix Versailles with UNESCO and UIA, 2019.
Architects Newspaper Best of Design Awards, 2019.
American Architecture Award, Chicago Athenaeum, 2019.
AIA Chicago Distinguished Building Award, 2019.

LEED Platinum Certified

the people's architect **carol ross barney**

"The design focuses on the interior by putting it on display. As famously exemplified by Apple, transparency connotes openness and accessibility ... The oversized roof canopy, hung with four, tastefully sized golden M's, is the kind of signage Mies van der Rohe could love."

The Architectural Review - Mimi Zeiger

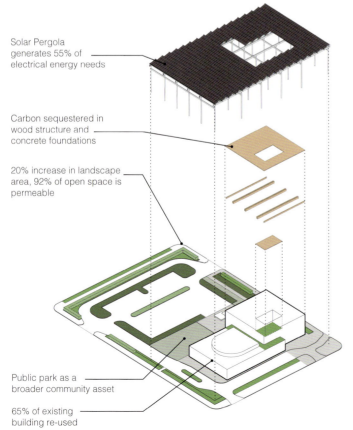

Solar Pergola generates 55% of electrical energy needs

Carbon sequestered in wood structure and concrete foundations

20% increase in landscape area, 92% of open space is permeable

Public park as a broader community asset

65% of existing building re-used

"...it was critical to feel a personal connection given the client-architect relationship takes time, energy, trust and commitment not just with the principal but with the entire staff. Carol stood out because of her genuine excitement, openness, curiosity and engagement which was infectious within her team and ours."

Max Carmona, AIA, former McDonald's Senior Director of Global Design & Development

the people's architect carol ross barney

"This temple of the Big Mac is billed as a model of energy-saving architecture - sustainability! It's supposed to bring people together - community! It even aims to be visually subtle, which amounts to a revolution..."

Blair Kamin - The Chicago Tribune's Pulitzer Prize Winning Architecture Critic

the people's architect carol ross barney

McDonald's Global Flagship at Walt Disney World

Lake Buena Vista, Florida

Description The McDonald's Flagship - Disney aims to become the world's first Net Zero Energy quick service restaurant and in doing so represents McDonald's commitment to building a better future.

Under a canopy clad in solar panels, the restaurant is a sustainable and healthy response to the Florida climate. Taking advantage of the humid subtropical climate, the building is naturally ventilated ~65% of the year. Jalousie windows, operated by outdoor humidity and temperature sensors, close automatically when air-conditioning is required. An outdoor "porch" features wood louvered walls and fans to create an extension of the indoor dining room.

As an energy intensive building typology and arguably an enabler of automobile culture, the McDonald's Flagship - Disney explores its role as a sustainable steward and learning lab for scalable technology; encouraging an industry to be more thoughtful, strategic, and impactful to a revolutionary degree.

Collaborative Partners CPH, Goodfriend Magruder, WSP, Schuler Shook

Size 8,024 sqft interior + 5,186 sqft porch

Completion 2020

Client McDonald's Corporation

Selected Recognition Fast Company World Changing Idea, 2021.
Planet Positive Award, Metropolis Magazine, 2021
American Architecture Award, The Chicago Athenaeum: Museum of Architecture and Design, 2021.
AIA Chicago Distinguished Building, 2020.

Net Zero Energy (seeking International Living Future Institute certification)

the people's architect carol ross barney

the people's architect **carol ross barney**

- 1,600 Photovoltaic panels
- 4,809 sqft glazing integrated photovoltaic panels
- 35% energy reduction on base building operations
- 1,800 sqft of green façade increases biodiversity
- Extensive "porch" creates comfortable outdoor dining
- Charred wood provides natural weather protection

Repairing the World 177 Selected Work — McDonald's Global Flagship at Walt Disney World

the people's architect **carol ross barney** 178

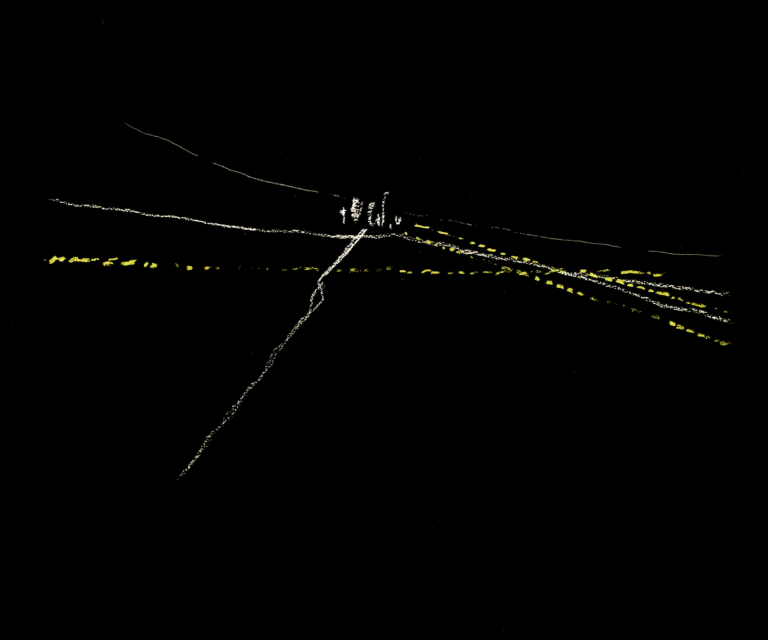

"You have to think about this amazing flat prairie that covers half the continent, meeting this amazing flat lake, one of the largest bodies of fresh water in the world. And at the intersection this great city, Chicago, grows. Our basic design premise is that design matters, and its not that it matters when you can afford it, or when it's convenient. Design matters all the time. Design Excellence, living in space that's truly appropriate, that's truly uplifting, isn't a privilege that only some people get. It's a right."

Sketch of Chicago and quote by Carol Ross Barney

Annex

Awards &
Publications

Architect Magazine: *What does being the first living woman to win the Gold Medal mean to you?*

Actually, I am the first living woman to win as an individual. Julia Morgan won posthumously. Denise Scott Brown and Angela Brooks who won with their partners are still very much alive.

I am very proud to be the person to break this barrier in recognizing the work of women architects. I am also sure that I am just the first of many.

Architect Magazine: Infrastructure of Hope, CTA Morgan Street Station by Katie Gerfen
April, 2013

"Last May, for the first time in more than 60 years, a train stopped at Morgan and Lake streets at the western edge of the Chicago Loop... As the neighborhood continues its resurgence... flexibility is key, but so was creating a design that is 'of its time,' Ross Barney says - as opposed to slipping the station invisibly into the urban fabric."

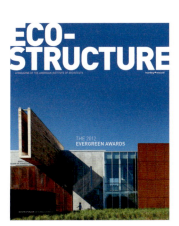

EcoStructure Magazine: 2012 Evergreen Awards, UMD Civil Engineering Building
2012

"This is one of the projects that attempted to respond and really reduce the water demand from an environmental standpoint... As water becomes ascendant as an issue to be dealt with, the fact that this building makes a narrative out of its water management is pretty terrific. And frankly, it's just a beautiful project."

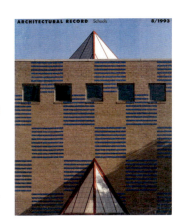

Architectural Record: Schools: Beacon for Learning by Charles D. Linn
August, 1993

"Providing color on the building in the form of bright masonry units, was a priority for architect Carol Ross Barney, who notes that many shopping mall exteriors provide a better model of what makes the exterior of a school appeal to children than do most school buildings."

Chicago Tribune Magazine: The People's Architect by Charles Leroux
May 30, 2004

"Carol Ross Barney's trademark sensitivity to human and environmental concerns is just one reason she is the People's Architect... She's a Chicago architect... from the modern movement of which Mies van der Rohe is the icon... It is this un-Miesian regard for intangibles that Thorne* finds unique. 'I think what sets her apart is her interest in the history of the site, how that place fits in the present and past memories of the community in which it will be built. And, of course, she's a pioneer...'"

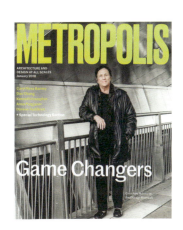

Metropolis: Carol Ross Barney is Chicago's New Daniel Burnham by Zach Mortice
January, 2018

"Ross Barney's tenacity has opened up a rare and enviable opportunity among architects. Here she is playing a distinct role in the conception and execution of a truly huge urban project. Like Burnham, Ross Barney's work has helped bend public policy and regulations to her will. The Riverwalk required an act of Congress to complete, and today 30 feet of public right-of-way is mandatory for development along the river... 'She's a genius...she brings people with her, which I think is a reflection of Burnham,' says Frisbie*."

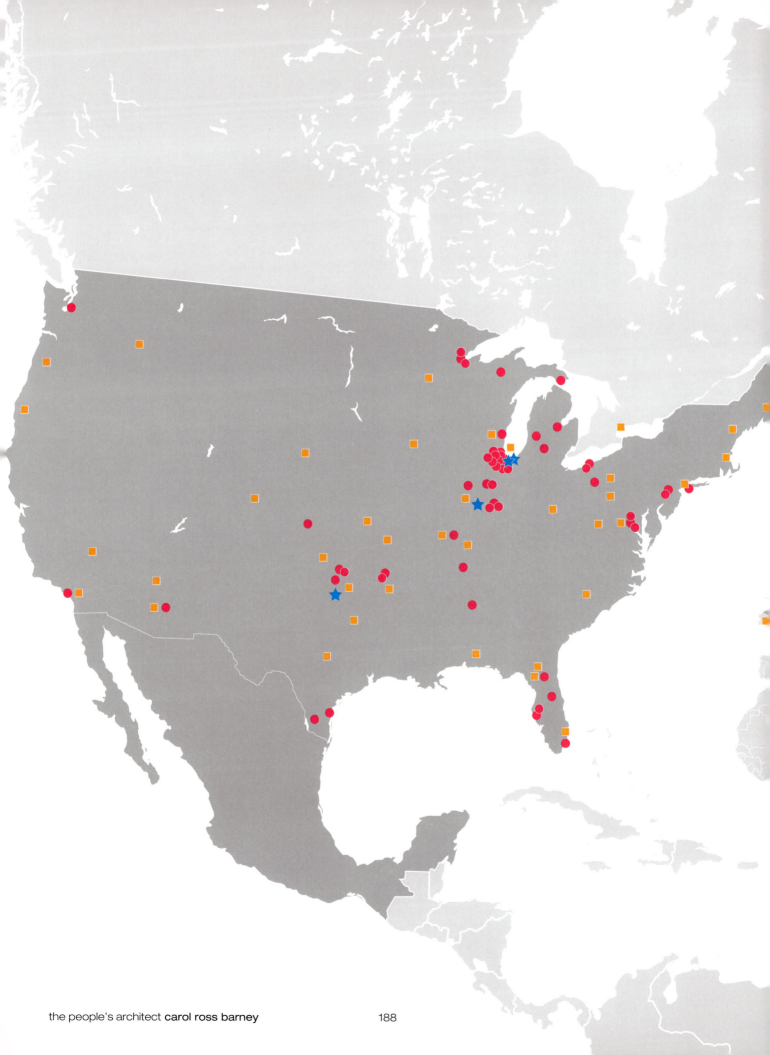

Carol Ross Barney is dedicated to designing public places and spaces. These efforts have produced a distinguished body of work with global influence.

Her **buildings and projects**, speculative and realized, span the globe and have been published in many languages. She has also **taught** and **lectured** at universities and institutions worldwide.

189 Annex — Awards & Publications

Life Story

above As an active member of AIA Chicago since 1974, Carol received their Lifetime Achievement Award in 2017. The AIA Chicago's women members of the College of Fellows gather at Carol Ross Barney's studio to celebrate the achievement.

the people's architect **carol ross barney**

Early Influences

Born in booming post war Chicago in 1949, Carol began her education in the Chicago Public School System. At age six her parents joined the waves of Americans seeking the suburban good life. Her earliest construction site memories are of the bi-level home built for her family in Northbrook, Illinois.

Attending an all-girls Catholic high school, Carol realized architecture presented an opportunity to make a meaningful improvement to people's quality of life. Inspired by John F. Kennedy's famous words, "ask not what your country can do for you, ask what you can do for your country", Carol felt an obligation to make some form of contribution to her surroundings and leave the world a better place. With the encouragement of her parents and guidance counselor (who had never advised a prospective architect), she enrolled at the University of Illinois Urbana Champaign, receiving a Bachelor of Architecture degree in 1971.

Service and Hope

A week after graduation, Carol and her husband, Alan Barney, a botanist, embarked on their assignment with the United States Peace Corps. Working with the fledgling Costa Rican National Park Service, their mission was to assist in the protection and preservation of Costa Rica's amazingly diverse and threatened ecology. Carol's projects included a master plan for coral reef protection at Parque Nacional Cahuita, restoration of the historic hacienda at Parque Nacional Santa Rosa, and worker housing at Parque Nacional Volcan Poas.

Following her service in the Peace Corps, Carol joined Holabird and Root. Shortly after joining, she received an invitation from Gertrude Lempp Kerbis, FAIA: "Come and meet other female architects re: Coalition - all invited". The group that convened that evening would found Chicago Women in Architecture; an organization that has become a leading advocacy group for women in the profession. As a founding member and first president, Carol embedded a sense of responsibility to seek equity for her peers, based not just on gender. During her tenure, which continues today in an advisory capacity, Carol served on the national AIA Women in Architecture Committee. She co-chaired a ground-breaking exhibition, titled "That Exceptional One: Women in American Architecture, 1888 - 1988", which commemorated the 100th anniversary of Louise Blanchard Bethune; the AIA's first woman to hold membership. The exhibition took its name from a 1955 article AIA Gold Medalist Pietro Belluschi, FAIA, wrote recommending that woman not pursue architecture due to its obstacles.

Noble Clients

At Holabird and Root, Carol met another mentor, John A. Holabird, FAIA. With John, Carol worked for what he called "noble clients", the ones with important cultural or social agendas but not necessarily the most money or high profile projects. The work ranged from the 1979 AIA Institute Honor Award winning restoration of the Chicago Public Library and Cultural Center to the Oakbrook Village Hall.

In 1981, Carol started a solo practice. Her first projects were for the "noble" clients she had worked with at Holabird and Root. In 1983, Carol received the Plym Traveling Fellowship from the

above Carol Ross Barney arrives in Costa Rica for United States Peace Corps service in 1971.

University of Illinois Urbana Champaign, which helped her to see the importance of building in the public realm, a belief that invigorated her work for years to come.

By the mid 1980's, Carol was awarded one of her first major commissions, the suburban Glendale Heights Post Office, which became an example of her willingness to rethink architectural conventions. Receiving a 1991 AIA Institute Honor Award for Architecture and a Presidential Design Award from the National Endowment of the Arts, the Post Office became a dazzling example of color, organization, and identity in the monotonous suburban context. Upon completion, it logged a 60% decrease in cooling load. While the United States Green Building Council had yet to be founded, the Post Office set a new precedent for environmentally conscious design.

Following the commission in Glendale Heights, Carol undertook a series of projects for Chicago Public Schools. The jobs were characterized by the challenges on which her studio's growing reputation was based: tough urban sites, communities facing complex social and economic challenges, and tight, inflexible government budgets. The first project, Cesar Chavez Multicultural Academic Center, was awarded a 1994 AIA Institute Honor Award for Architecture. Upon its completion and success, the school district asked Carol to replicate the building on a different site. Refusing to do so, she convinced the client to allow her to design a school that spoke specifically to the site and community it would serve. Completed in 1996, Little Village Academy was honored with two Institute Honor Awards, one for Interior Architecture in 1999, the other for Architecture in 2002. Praised for its ability to articulate bold forms and generate inspirational environments, Little Village gained national acclaim and was featured in an AIA Commercial Campaign.

The People's Architect

In 1997, Carol was chosen as the lead designer for the Oklahoma City Federal Building, the first female architect to head the design of such a commission. Following the devastating bombing of the Alfred P. Murrah Building by an act of domestic terrorism in 1995, the General Services Administration was tasked with developing standards for the protection of government facilities. The building was both the philosophical and practical response to tragedy, with the main design

above right Carol received the AIA Gold Medal in 2023. Pictured with AIA President Emily Grandstaff Rice and Vice President and CEO Lakisha Woods on stage during the AIA Conference on Architecture, A'23.
above In 2005, Carol received the AIA's Award for Public Architecture. Pictured with Douglas Steidl, FAIA and Norman L. Koonce, FAIA.

objective being to create a secure space. Carol has continued to work closely with the General Services Administration on these topics during subsequent federal commissions.

In 2005 Carol was Awarded the Award for Public Architecture from the American Institute of Architects. The jury noted that her "career demonstrates a strong sensitivity, care, and compassion for the public. Her projects not only listen and respond to users' needs, they also dignify them." That same year, the Chicago Architectural Foundation mounted a transformational exhibition: "5 Architects". The show became one of the first to focus on women architects, presenting the work of Carol Ross Barney, Zaha Hadid, Julie Snow, and Jeanne Gang.

From buildings that enrich communities to infrastructure and urban systems that influence a city's fabric, her work with the Chicago Transit Authority (CTA) has touched nearly a third of the system, and has welcomed millions of Chicagoans. The first in a series of new inter-system stations to be constructed in more than 30 years, Morgan Street Station became an instant success. So too did Cermak McCormick Place Station, which now greets millions of first time visitors and neighborhood residents as they enter the Near South Side. Thanks to Carol's work and advocacy, project types often left to function and the bottom line have yielded compelling arguments for why design matters.

For the last 15 years, Carol has been leading a movement to regenerate the Chicago River. Throughout the process, Carol and the city have worked to think beyond conventions of civic space, designing a progressive urban park, the Chicago Riverwalk. Her influence has allowed for the exploration of new relations between city and river; an interwoven coexistence of nature and man. The space has won numerous awards and has been the topic of case-studies by cities world wide. When the final phase opened in the fall of 2016, the culmination of

a plan drafted by Daniel Burnham in 1909 was realized in the contemporary context of Carol's urban thinking.

Civic Bent
In 2013, Carol was elected to the Board of Governors of the Metropolitan Planning Council (MPC). The Council's goal is to solve today's pressing planning challenges and prepare Chicago for the needs of the future. As part of this service, she was appointed by Chicago Mayor Rahm Emanuel to the Great Rivers Chicago Leadership Commission, which created the first cohesive vision for all three of Chicago's Rivers, in collaboration with her studio. This work influenced an exhibition, "Chicago River Edge Ideas Lab", at the 2017 Chicago Architecture Biennial, which featured the work of nine international teams, including Ross Barney Architects, Field Operations, Studio Gang, and others. The prompt was to envision the extension of the Chicago Riverwalk south and has helped set the stage for engineering guidelines. Carol has been a strong contributor.

Underlying an interest in great design, Carol has had an unyielding commitment to the policy of excellence and innovation in publicly funded projects. She called the Village of Wilmette, Illinois, home from 1978 - 2009 and served on the Economic Development Commission, Plan Commission, and as Chair of the Appearance Review Commission. Carol has served numerous organizations dedicated to architecture, urban design, and entrepreneurship including the Board of Directors for the Chicago Architecture Foundation (now the Chicago Architecture Center), the Chicago Network, Cliff Dwellers, and AIA Chicago.

Environmental Stewardship
Carol's early adoption of sustainable principles pre-dates the trend of LEED and is embedded in all of her work. With a portfolio of Net Zero and Platinum, Gold and Silver LEED certified

the people's architect **carol ross barney**

buildings, her studio has a proven track record of environmental practice. In recent years, the AIA's Committee on the Environment has honored Carol's work with two Top 10 Awards.

The Oklahoma City Federal Building and the Sault Ste. Marie Border Station are early examples of a rigorous commitment to sustainable practices by the General Services Administration. To this day, the Border Station is still one of the most environmentally conscious to be built. The adoption of formal policies and standards for federal projects were formulated after these projects were completed, undoubtedly influenced by Carol's work.

In 2008, The Jewish Reconstructionist Congregation Synagogue in Evanston, Illinois, became the first house of worship to achieve LEED Platinum certification. The congregation's desire for Tikkun Olam, Hebrew for repairing the world, and a tight budget, drove the inventive design that turned a spiritual relationship into a sustainable commitment.

More recently Carol has brought this passion for the environment to a global corporation: McDonald's. These collaborations have resulted in LEED Platinum and Net Zero Energy buildings; transforming the brand through design, stewardship, and contributions to the city's urban fabric.

Educator and Mentor
Carol has combined teaching with practice since 1976 when she taught at the University of Illinois at Chicago. During a 40 year academic career, she has taught at the University of Oklahoma where she was the Bruce Goff Visiting Chair and at the Illinois Institute of Technology, where she has been an adjunct professor since 1994. Topics of her studio courses have been interrelated to the architectural explorations of her practice, from water transportation to mixed use developments advocating for a renaissance in light manufacturing. Her students have gone on to win prestigious awards, recognizing the value of their design provocations. Additionally she has served on the Board of Overseers for both her alma mater, the University of Illinois at Urbana Champaign, and the Illinois Institute of Technology.

Talented cohorts have passed through her studio as employees. They have gone on to build successful architectural practices, have become clients and university architects, and have flourished in alternative careers based on the values Carol instilled, further distributing a work ethic and commitment to an architect's social responsibility.

People Not at the Table
Carol's design process is one of inclusivity. Empowered by a sense of responsibility, she has chosen to fight for the collective aspirations of society. This confidence exists on a sense of ownership; that she too will use the spaces she designs and interacts with. By representing those values, interests, and aspirations, Carol lends an assertive voice to the conversation that is not typically present. Pushing public and private clients is a fine line to tread, full of headaches and battles. What some might consider everyday spaces that do not need to be designed, often have an inestimable impact on quality of life. These are the spaces Carol cares deeply about. It is this belief that makes her the "People's Architect".

AIA Gold Medal
Carol received the 2023 American Institute of Architects Gold Medal, recognizing individuals whose work has had a lasting influence on the theory and practice of architecture. The AIA wrote "An unrivaled architect for the people, Barney exudes design excellence, social responsibility, and generosity. Throughout all of her work, she has endeavored to make the world a better place."

Studio Members

Carol Ross Barney
Mary Welsh
Caren Redish
James Jankowski
Champ Maxey
Suzanne Gubitz
Donald Tomes
Michael Breclaw
Elaine Topousis
Michelle Kowalski
William Heckel
Barabara Corbine
Stan Grecowicz
James Sarahiecki
Joel Lome
Bonnie Stewart
Catherine Lee
Heather McTammany
Kenneth Sproul
Frank Michalski
Paul Pedtke
Claudia Ledwich
Susan Kvasnicka
Mary O'Toole
Edward Ehlert
Amy Schutz
Judith Weirauch
Cheryl Dodson
John Fried
Michael Chastain
Cheryl Combs-Grabill
Thomas Raveret
Laura Saviano
Karen Fletcher
Sally Levine
Michael Roach
Michael Wemhoff
Katherine Kalewski
Daniel Miller
Meredith Dytch
Gary Green
Lisa Brown
John Kouchoukos
Daniel McIsaac
Fay Kyroudis
Kay Vierk Janis
Jenny Greiner
Wesley Hoover
James Butz
Patricia Natke
Loralie Chastain

Susan Budinsky
Chris Gazso
Jeffrey Peck
Robin Savage
Alice Combs
Allison Fultz
Lavetha Green
Martin Lockwood-Bean
Alan Kirkpatrick
David Kuhlman
Edward Young
Michael Petti
Carol Schmidt
Deborah Burkhart
Richard Podgorny
Elizabeth Nickerson
Terri Donaldson
Sallie Schwartzkopf
Elizabeth Purdy
Brian O'Neal
Christopher Mazzier
Eric Martin
Joon-Gul Oh
Shannon Sanders
Marilyn Dobbs
Robert Hillery
Ellen Malmon
Lacey Bailey
Steven Tousey
Sandra Brown
Robert Finigan
Maria Pimentel
Kevin O'Connor
Ferdinanda Marcic
Kevin Loftus
Victor Lopez
Michelle Gerstner
Kent Davidson
J. Michael Kilpatrick
Amelia Thomas
Dana Guler
Stacey Taylor
Rozi Yusoff
Adam Koziol
Stephen Katz
Melissa Tekulve
Michael Siciliano
Jenny Ro
Miriam Neet
Laura Parisi
Kim Everts

Michael Ross
Andrew Volckens
Mayra Era Werner
Sung-Jin Byun
Mariangely Rivera
Kimberly Wilson
Emily Basham
David Parisi
Daniel Pohrte
Christopher Moore
Ripal Patel
Arthur Cantwell
Krista Jiannacopoulos
Ross Barney
Amy Holz
David C. Wickstrom
Teresa Jack
Krystyna Dakof
Curtis Jones, Jr.
Donna Long
LaTasha Brown
Eric Davis
George Matos
Christine Chan
Sonia Johansen
Aaron Howe-Cornelison
Tiffany Nash
Cayl Hollis
Jody Luna
Stephanie Witherspoon
Gaily Demakakos
Jim Hurtubise
Alexandra Kowerko
Derek Dinkeloo
Eve Fineman
Margaret Russo
Susan Mitchell
Mario Rosado
Albert Shaw
Young Chai
Ronald Brueckmann
Hilary Padget
Eva Wang
Chantelle Brewer
Shinya Uehara
Jung Mo
Ruchita Varma
George Kugler
Robert Krotser
Aisha Edwards
David Cintron

Carl Bergamini
Steve Stone
Andrew Schachman
Colin Craig
Todd Wendell
Eric Robinson
James Criss
Rebecca Beaulieu
Amy Totten
Susan Otteman
Brent Foster
Kimberley Patten
Christopher Martin
Mark Verwoerdt
Monica Chadha
Jonathan Graves
Amy Preston
Michael Nichols
Pamela Walker
Erica Warshawsky
Cynthia Smith
Rajiv Pinto
Marc Anderson
Roxanne Henry
Huili Feng
Darya Minosyants
Sung-Joon Kim
Ohin Kwon
Ricardo Nabholz
Steven Rohr
Tatsuya Iwata
Craig Hamilton
Emily Brown
Jonathan Wlodaver
Ryan Giblin
Sean Schrader
Kim Sagami
John Barney
Stephen Schoener
Jasmine Santiago
Andrew Vesselinovitch
Mordecai Scheckter
Iffat Afsana
Anna Ninoyu
Dmitry Barsky
Kim Sagami
Nicolas Sanchez
Krisjan Gorospe
Aaron Garbutt
Krista Simons Gliva
David C Erven

Megan Burbank
Amy Chun
Darryl Mallett
Ryan Gann
Jose Quintero Lopez
Nora Erickson
Youngjae Lee
Lindsey Telford
Wendy Anderhous
Ryan Docken
Itzi Velazquez-Becerril
Yifan Liang
Jason Vogel
Jeremy Gentile
Kevin Taylor
Misa Inoue
Naila Opiangah
Marcus Malesh
Cesar Pacheco
Sarah Bruketta
Jhilmil Jha
Amy Shouder
Annie Ball
Kia Jones
Quoc Trung Nigel Van Ha
Lena Reiff
Barrett Peterson
Elizabeth Inman
Casey Ryan
Beckett Anderhous-Custer
Victor Torres
Angela Vezzaro
Ruchi Dattani
Dongseop Mike Shin
Claire Wagner
Ilyssa Kaserman
Dylan King
Shoko Nakamura
Delia Otero
Meita Arethusa
Paridhi Agarwal
Regine Antenor
Charlotte Cox
Lauren Eaton
Joshua Ascencio
Jackie Guataquira
Bryan Cruz Lopez
Christine Robillard
Robert Prochaska
Kathleen Bailey
Gisella Nicho

Contributors

Iker Gil

Iker Gil is the founder of MAS Studio, Editor in Chief of the nonprofit MAS Context, and Executive Director of the SOM Foundation. Iker has edited or coedited several books including *Radical Logic: On the Work of Ensamble Studio* and *Shanghai Transforming*. He has curated multiple exhibitions including Nocturnal Landscapes, Poured Architecture: Sergio Prego on Miguel Fisac, and BOLD: Alternative Scenarios for Chicago, part of the inaugural Chicago Architecture Biennial. He was Associate Curator of the US Pavilion for the 2018 Venice Architecture Biennale and co-curator of Exhibit Columbus 2020–2021. He has taught at the School of the Art Institute of Chicago (SAIC), University of Illinois at Chicago (UIC), Illinois Institute of Technology (IIT), and Escola da Cidade (São Paulo).

Oscar Riera Ojeda

Oscar Riera Ojeda is an editor and designer based in the US, China, and Argentina. Born in 1966, in Buenos Aires, he moved to the United States in 1990. Since then, he has published over three hundred books, assembling a remarkable body of work notable for its thoroughness of content, timeless character, and sophisticated and innovative craftsmanship. Oscar Riera Ojeda's books have been published by many prestigious publishing houses across the world, including Birkhäuser, Byggförlaget, The Monacelli Press, Gustavo Gili, Thames & Hudson, Rizzoli, Damiani, Page One, ORO Editions, Whitney Library of Design, and Taschen. Oscar Riera Ojeda is also the creator of numerous architectural book series, including Ten Houses, Contemporary World Architects, The New American House and The New American Apartment, Architecture in Detail, and Single Building. His work has received many international awards, in-depth reviews, and citations. He is a regular contributor and consultant for several publications in the field. In 2001 Oscar Riera Ojeda founded ORO Editions, a company at which he was responsible for the completion of nearly one hundred titles. In 2008 he established his current publishing venture, Oscar Riera Ojeda Publishers, a firm with fifteen employees and locations across three continents.

Photography Credits

Kate Joyce Studios
Cover, pages 14-15, top page 17, bottom right page 19, 24-25, 27-29, 31-32, 34-37, 74-75, 77-79, 82-91, 93-96, 98-101, 103-107, 108-111, 136-137, 149-156, 173-181.

John Boehm Photography
Page 7.

Ross Barney Architects
Page 16, bottom page 18, top and bottom left page 19, 80, top page 121, 190-192.

Kendall McCaugherty, Hall+Merrick+McCaugherty
Pages 8-9, 47-51, 54-59, 61-62, 64-73, 113-117, 119, 120-121, 124-127, 157, 159, 160-171, 198-199.

Whitten Sabbatini Photographer
Bottom page 17.

Matt Wargo Photography
Pages 20-21.

Nate Moser
Pages 52-53.

Alan Tansey Photographer
Pages 2-3, 118, 122-123.

Tara White Photographer
Top page 18.

© Chicago History Museum, Hedrich Blessing Collection, Steve Hall Photographer
Pages 39-45,139-141, 144-147, 142-143.

Brad Feinknopf Photography
Pages 129-135

Chloe Jackman Photography
Page 193.

"Parallel Histories" CAB 5,
located on the future site of DuSable Park.
Photo by Kendall McCaugherty.

Book Credits

Graphic Design by Florencia Damilano
Art Direction by Oscar Riera Ojeda
Copy Editing by Kit Maude

Laura Saviano, Principal, Ross Barney Architects
Ryan Gann, AIA, Producer

OSCAR RIERA OJEDA
PUBLISHERS

Copyright © 2024 by Oscar Riera Ojeda Publishers Limited
ISBN 978-1-946226-63-1
Published by Oscar Riera Ojeda Publishers Limited
Printed in China

Oscar Riera Ojeda Publishers Limited
Unit 1331, Beverley Commercial Centre,
87-105 Chatham Road South, Tsim Sha Tsui, Kowloon, Hong Kong

Production Offices
Suit 19, Shenyun Road,
Nanshan District, Shenzhen 518055, China

International Customer Service & Editorial Questions: +1-484-502-5400

www.oropublishers.com | www.oscarrieraojeda.com
oscar@oscarrieraojeda.com

All rights reserved. No part of this book may be reproduced, stored in a retrieval system, or transmitted in any form or by any means, including electronic, mechanical, photocopying or microfilming, recording, or otherwise (except that copying permitted by Sections 107 and 108 of the U.S. Copyright Law and except by reviewers for the public press) without written permission from the publisher.